3 August 1986

Happy *[illegible]* W
Henry —
an uncommon,
sensible human, and
cherished friend.
Bob & Merce

Kim Willia

BOOK O
UNCOMM
SENS

Kim Williams'

BOOK OF
UNCOMMON
SENSE

A Practical Guide
With 10 Rules
For Nearly Everything

HPBooks

I'd like to express my sincere thanks to the following for their very considerable aid and encouragement:

All Things Considered
Bitterroot Educational Resources
Warren Brier
Bob Cushman
Ron Erickson
Phil Hess
Charles Hood
Journalism School Typing Room (UM)
William Kittredge
KUFM
William Marcus
The Missoulian
The Montana Standard
National Public Radio
DMR, Proteus, Inc.
Schenkman Publishing Co., Inc.
Art Silverman
Susan Stamberg
Barbara Tucker
University of Montana
and last, but of course not least,
Mel Williams, my husband

Published by HPBooks, Inc.
P.O. Box 5367
Tucson, AZ 85703
602/888-2150
ISBN: 0-89586-378-2
Library of Congress Catalog No. 85-81842
©1986 HPBooks, Inc.
Printed in U.S.A.
1st Printing

Publisher: Rick Bailey
Editorial Director: Theodore DiSante
Art Director: Don Burton
Cover Design: Leslie Sinclair
Typography: Cindy Coatsworth, Michelle Carter
Director of Manufacturing: Anthony B. Narducci

Contents

Health

You have to do it yourself.
Doctors and hospitals are all around you,
but in the long run
your health is in your own hands.

"Kim, don't ever get into a nursing home,"
a nurse said to me. "We have a name
for people like you. We call you difficult
and feed you a double dose
of tranquilizers."

That's what I mean—you have to do
before you are done to.

I took up cross-country skiing last year—when I was 61. A friend put her extra pair of skis on my feet and said, "Now do it."

And I did do it. I fell over my own feet and I tumbled into snowbanks, but in one month I was flying down Moose Ridge. Well, not exactly flying. I was sometimes snowplowing, sometimes leaning on my poles, and sometimes wondering what I was doing up there with the moose. But I loved it.

You may wonder why I didn't take up cross-country skiing 20 years ago? Or 30? Or 40? The answer is that I'm in better shape now than I was 20 or 30 or 40 years ago.

I had to make some real changes to get that way. I even weighed 160 pounds once. But I'm not necessarily a "thinner-is-better" person. In fact, I am always on the verge of being a bit overweight. I'm five feet two and weigh 127, which is OK with me, but I tend to creep upward. And well, I *am* an eater: "Kim Williams, I saw you eat a brownie!" Oh dear.

So I have to watch my weight. But that's only part of what I mean when I say I'm in better shape now than I was all those years ago. What I really mean is that I can do a lot more now than before. That's the main difference.

I can play tennis, then walk (I don't drive) to the university—about a mile—do whatever I have to do, walk home, and then if I have an evening class (to teach or take) I can walk to the university again.

And I rarely get colds. Sometimes I go for two years without getting a cold. That's what I mean by being in shape. I don't mean that someone is going to whistle at me.

Now, why should I care about this shape or state of health I'm in? Well, I think Darwin's survival of the fittest is in vogue again. It sort of left for a while, but I think it's back.

Every day you hear about a new pollution, a new additive, a new preservative that has been doing us wrong. And how about all those that no one has found out about yet?

Can you get away from these substances? It's tough. They're in the air, in the water, in your soup, your vegetables, fruit, eggs and milk. So what can you do?

I figure that the better shape you're in, the better off you are. Yes, there are doctors, hospitals and health insurance plans. But the fact is that I'm scared of all of them a bit, too.

Wasn't there a drug for diabetes that cured the diabetes but killed the patient? I wrote a poem about that. It isn't an epic poem—it has only two lines:

> *They cured his ill*
> *but killed poor Will.*

That's the way it has been with more than one "magic cure."

So I say that the best thing I can do for myself is to take responsibility for my health. I must put my body into the best shape I can. First, so I can stay away from medicine, doctors, hospitals—all of that. And second, so I can successfully resist the odd substances we have around us. Germs, too, of course. It works the same for them. There are people who can be right in the middle of typhoid and not get it. There are people who work with poisonous chemicals and live as if they were immune. I want to be like them.

If we can't hope to get rid of all the odd substances we have in, on and around us, we have to say to our bodies—"BE STRONG."

For example, I was eating sprayed cherries last summer. I knew they'd been sprayed six or seven times. Maybe the rain washed the spray off. Maybe it didn't. So I said to myself, "Cells of my body, gird your loins because I'm going to feast on these cherries and who knows what has been done to them."

If you are a student of eastern philosophy, you might say I'm revving up my yin and yang, or my electric field. However you want to look at it, it comes down to this: You have to give your body all the help you can—with exercise and with food that has been tampered with as little as possible.

And then there's your spirit. You have to rev up your spirit to do battle. I almost believe that might be the most important part. Health is good bones and muscles, but you also need a fire burning in your center. Call it *spirit,* call it *mind*—even *psyche* or *soul.* You'll see what I mean as you read on.

Fire the Doctor, If Necessary

I fired the doctor by letter rather than face to face. Oh, miserable coward that I was—tears running down my face—I knew I'd dissolve if I went to his office. After all, a doctor is next door to God. Didn't we all grow up with that? To doubt the doctor is to make one lost and lonely in the universe.

Nevertheless, I fired the doctor:

Dear Doctor,
Hold everything. Cancel everything. It's my lump. It's my groin.

I also enclosed a poem I wrote while I was tramping through the snow one day. The doctor was a friend of mine. We went to the same church. I liked him. So I sent him the poem with the letter for him to understand that this was not a matter undertaken lightly. I was nervous, shaking all over, and I couldn't eat. I wanted somebody to hold my hand and take over—a kindly, white-haired doctor, or father, or God.

I wanted all that, but I couldn't do it. I have this picture of somebody lying in a hospital bed, people coming and going, tests here, tests there, charts and maps and hypodermic needles, trays, bedpans. And nobody ever asks you anything except "Isn't this a fine day, Kim?" They use your first name as if you were a five-year-old child. And you never make another decision.

Now understand that I'm not knocking everything about doctors, hospitals and the medical profession. A doctor set my brother's arm; one fixed my husband's prostate; one probably even saved my life. I had blood poisoning once, at least that's what they called it in the '30s. My foot swelled, then my knee swelled. The doctor said as he cut a huge cross in my knee, "You were almost a goner." Thank you Dr. Wicks.

I have great faith in doctors repairing the machinery of the body. But repairing is not the same as healing. I have another picture in my mind: Me trying to keep the doctor from pulling my body apart from my soul. He's dealing with the machinery of my body, and I'm trying to hold everything together.

I fired the doctor because I had to think. I didn't want a biopsy in two days. Maybe I didn't want one at all. What would I do if the biopsy results were positive? In whose hands did I want to be?

So I took a month to think. I walked in the snow (it was winter); I climbed a mountain; maybe I even prayed.

I finally decided—oh, the nerve!—that my lump was not cancer and I might as well go to the hospital and find that out.

I couldn't go back to my first doctor. He'd say, "You waited a MONTH?"

I needed a new start, with a new, young—shall I say malleable—doctor. I chose a young surgeon and said to him, "I want local anesthesia."

"Fine," the surgeon said. That's what he said, and that's what I got, but it turned out that I had to pay for a full knockout. "Well, you know, Mrs. Williams (they got around to that finally), we can't take a chance on a person of your age. Full anesthesia has to be on standby."

It was no fun with the local anesthesia. I was awake; I felt things. But I wanted to know what was being done. If it had turned out that a biopsy was necessary (actually it was a peculiar hernia) I wanted to know and be there at the scene, so to speak.

Also I recuperated much faster. I didn't even stop at the recovery room. "I want my lunch," I said.

If my lump had been cancer, before I went one step further, I would have wanted some real facts. I'd want to know how many cases of this type of cancer had received Treatment A, how many years the patients lived and what quality of life it was, versus how many cases had received Treatment B, Treatment C and so forth.

Even information about the laying on of hands—don't forget that. Or Megavitamins or Norman Cousins' type of treatment. Remember that he signed himself right out of the hospital and did all kinds of unorthodox things. He recovered and wrote about it in his book *Anatomy of an Illness.*

And how about doing nothing at all? What are the odds on that working as well as any of the above?

That's what I needed a month for. It was my body; my life. How could I just lay it on a table and say, "Do with me what you will?" Maybe in things like cancer the doctor's judgment might not be any better than my own. A doctor friend of mine once told me, "Sometimes you have to guess in 50 percent of your diagnoses."

And I can't forget when I had hepatitis in South America. The doctor at the American Embassy told my husband—not me—"Your wife has an allergy. Get this prescription filled." He drank a scotch with my husband and left.

I had to think about all this. A month was hardly enough. Because didn't I have to make up my own mind whether I could live with my lump? If it was cancer—well, I had to make my own decision.

I guess what I want from the medical profession are more facts right out in the open. Really, I want to be able to go to the public library and find a machine with all of the statistics in it. Push a button and get a computer printout. On cancer, on prostate operations, open-heart surgery—even aspirins. How many people died from aspirins last year?

Why We Need Shamans

When you break your leg
a doctor can set it,
but who can find the fairy,
the spirit, the elf, the troll,
who broke your leg
and lives inside of you
and next time may break your head?

I read somewhere that in some primitive cultures when an accident happens, the shaman (a kind of medicine man) fixes the leg or head or whatever, but that is considered only half the service. The other half is finding and fixing the *why*.

We're all familiar with the modern methods:

"Doctor, why did my son's leg break?"

"Take this prescription to the drugstore. Two pills twice a day after meals."

"Doctor, Rodney broke his arm last year."

"Come back in a week."

"Doctor, Rodney sprained his collarbone two years ago."

"Don't you worry, young lady. We'll soon have your son as good as new."

Oh, sometimes, I do long for a shaman.

A Questionnaire for Doctors

My friend Trixie, an ex-nurse, was talking to a doctor who treats mental problems. Trixie asked him what he thought of psychonutrition. That's the idea that what you put in your stomach has something to do with your mental state.

The doctor answered, "I don't see anything in that theory."

"Well," I said to Trixie, "I certainly think that anyone who goes to that doctor for treatment should know that." I added as a kind of afterthought, "Doctors ought to fill out a questionnaire just as we do when we go for treatment."

I said it kiddingly, but after thinking it over I don't see why it shouldn't be done. Why shouldn't doctors fill out a questionnaire? Don't the patients have to answer all kinds of questions, some very embarrassing? But who has the courage to ask a doctor, "Look, how do you feel about back pain? Would you opt for surgery? Would you opt for injections? Medicines? Exercise? All things being equal, which treatment would *you* choose?"

So now I'm designing a questionnaire for doctors, dentists and therapists—maybe especially for therapists—in case I need one. I want to know their viewpoints on health and health care.

What started me thinking about a questionnaire was not only Trixie's experience. I was talking to a therapist at a party and I asked him, "Have you ever worked with cutting down on the sugar intake of some of your patients. Uh, pardon me, clients?"

He looked sheepish. "I'm a sugar freak myself," he answered.

Another thing that happened was a discussion with a physical-education professor at the University of Montana when my husband had "slipped disk" trouble. "You choose your treatment by choosing your doctor," Brian said. "If you choose a surgeon, you are more likely to be operated on than if you choose a non-surgeon. If the doctor you choose is a believer in injections or medicines, you're more likely to go that route. If your doctor is like me, he'll try an exercise program first."

If we had gone on, we probably would have covered, "If you find a doctor who believes 'You are what you eat,' he might prescribe changing your way of eating."

I'm still working on my questionnaire. I'm designing the questions so they'll be easy to answer, but will tell us patients what we need to know to choose. "Ha!" you might say, "no doctor will put one check mark on your questionnaire." Well, we might have to wait a while, but perhaps not too long. More and more doctors are graduating every year. Some of the younger ones just might go along.

Opposite is the latest version:

Questionnaire for Doctors
(Please check True or False.)

1) Hamburger, French fries and soda is not a bad lunch.

2) The holistic health movement is overrated.

3) I don't have time to exercise.

4) Aerobic exercise is a marvelous thing.

5) I skip breakfast often.

6) I don't believe that the food a person eats has much to do with mental outlook.

7) Too much unnecessary surgery is being performed.

8) Doctors—our healers—are just as prone to drug and alcohol addiction as the general population.

9) I am more comfortable with the old-fashioned doctor-patient relationship.

10) This questionnaire is unfair to the medical establishment.

(I would pick a doctor who answered false to all but 4, 7 and 8.)

A Questionnaire for Patients

"They never have just one operation," Trixie said. "They're always back to get something else done."

"Good heavens," I said. "Does it start a chain reaction?"

All of a sudden my hands flew in the air and my next words came out in verse form. This happens with me—as if I were suddenly on a soapbox. I'm not even sure where the words come from. Once I changed my life overnight simply because I wrote a poem. "You are a mudpond, stagnant," I wrote. And the next day I went to New York and got a serious job—I mean I started looking for one.

So when Trixie said to me, "It's one operation and then another," I immediately saw Arfy standing in front of me. Arfy doesn't exist, but don't you know someone like him?

> *Arfy had bladder trouble.*
> *They reamed out his something.*
> *He got scar tissue—*
> *they reamed him out again.*
> *He became incontinent,*
> *had to wear a diaper, got a rash.*
> *Now he's on Maxi-thins,*
> *Johnson's baby powder, and*
> *Helena Rubenstein's honey and almond*
> *moisturizer lotion.*

This questionnaire is for *you*. It's your head, heart, bladder or liver. The object is to find the answer to the question: "Is this surgery necessary?" Be honest now.

Pre-Surgery Questionnaire for Patients

1) Am I looking for a shortcut solution? (Yes, I know—shortCUT.) Andy Capp in his comic strip (comic strips are a kind of window on our world) once said the same thing very precisely. His doctor said to him: "Andy, your liver is deteriorating. You have to cut down on your drinking."

Andy said to the doctor, "Can't you operate?"

I remember when our newspaper here in Missoula once had a big feature on post-open-heart-surgery therapy. "Did you ever see people who looked so much alike?" I asked Mel. "These six men are practically identical. Every one is overweight. Here they are in the therapy unit jumping rope, jogging, no doubt weighing their food by ounces. Why didn't they do it *before* the operation? Who's paying the bill, and what is it doing to *my* insurance rates?"

I also remember when I walked into my precinct voting place the year I was a judge. After looking around at the other workers I said, "My Lord, I'm in the Valley of the Fatties." There were three women—and not one was under 180 pounds. We spent the day talking recipes. The one who came with five women's magazines and chocolate chip cookies for breakfast confided that she'd had her stomach stapled shut.

"Can you eat?" I asked.

"Only half a cup at a time."

Into that half a cup she put a hot dog, baked beans, French fries, chocolate cake, fried chicken and four soft drinks.

"Did the doctors recommend anything like Overeaters Anonymous?" I asked in a small voice.

"Never heard of them."

I didn't ask who paid for the operation and what it was doing to my insurance rates. Maybe next time.

2) Of course I'm getting a second opinion, but is this second opinion by someone unrelated to the first opinion? And do I need a third opinion?

3) Am I having this operation because someone else is paying 80 percent of it? Would I have it if I were paying 80 percent? 100 percent? Even 50 percent?

Don't Do Me That Favor

Please, Oh mighty government,
don't give me 100% free health care.
I know myself. I'll have a leg set
when it isn't even broken.
I'll fill up my medicine cabinet
with every pill, ointment, capsule
and salve in the drugstore.
I'll get monkey-gland injections
from Rumania, voodoo potions from
Haiti. I'll have symptoms
of every major—and minor—
ailment known to man.
Oh God, protect me from myself.

4) Given that all operations have some risk—i.e., I may not wake up or I may wake up crooked or shriveled or in a coma—is this operation worth the risk?

5) Am I exchanging one set of ills for another set—i.e., a pain in the lower back is gone, but now I can't walk very well?

6) Am I having this operation because I don't have anything better to do? The hospital is warm and comfortable, and people bring

you fruit and flowers. The doctor says don't worry, the insurance will cover it, and damn it (!) my only sister went to Sun City and Santa Barbara and didn't invite me along. Serves her right if she has to come back and take care of me.

7) Have I waited a proper length of time to see if things get better by themselves? They sometimes do, you know. A farmer here in the Bitterroot Valley was scheduled for open-heart surgery, but he had a crisis on his farm so he postponed the operation. After the crisis ended the farmer said, "My God, I feel OK." He called the doctor and said, "I'll stay the way I am."

My friend Marilyn Walker in Lancaster, Ohio, wrote to me that her body—all by itself—rejected a tumor. It rejected and ejected the tumor right out of her uterus. "The gynecologist said he had never seen that happen," Marilyn wrote. "He had urged me for four years to have a hysterectomy, but I'd refused."

That's exactly why I wrote in my poem to the doctor I fired:

> Dear Doctor, I love you
> but I'll take the miracle first.

8) Am I sending a cannon to kill a fly? It wasn't long ago that tonsils were attacked as if they were a foreign body. After two sore throats, out they went.

9) Is this operation a trophy for me? I really do believe there are people who pursue an operation like a rare blue butterfly to be captured, mounted and hung on the wall.

"I bet you're wondering why I didn't go to Greece," said a local gentleman whom I will call Thomas. As he was telling me, he drew himself up (Can I say proudly? Surely not. But he did draw himself up.) and said, "I had a triple bypass."

"Oh," I said. That's all I had to say. Thomas went on. "I went to the best cardiologists here in Missoula. They said I didn't need an operation."

Was Thomas happy, contented, relieved? Read on.

"My wife insisted that I go to San Francisco and be examined there. That's where I had the operation."

I had the feeling that if the "best" cardiologists in San Francisco had decided against operating, Thomas and his wife would have gone to Houston, and from there to the Mayo Clinic, from there to Boston, not stopping until he got what he obviously wanted.

10) Am I someone else's trophy?

You, my lucky friend,
could be the GRAND WINNER of the
FIRST ARTIFICIAL
BRAIN TRANSPLANT

How To Survive Your Hospital Stay

When my husband went to the hospital, I sent these 10 guidelines with him:

10 Hospital Hints

1) Ask the doctor if you can get off the liquid diet faster than usual. Tell him you are accustomed to a high-fiber diet and you don't want to become constipated and then have to take laxatives.

2) Ask nurses for any of the following drinks at any hour (they are kept in a little room on the floor): apricot nectar, grapefruit juice, prune juice, tomato juice, lowfat milk, tea, decaffeinated coffee, hot chocolate. When you are feeling better, you can help yourself.

3) Don't forget to drink plain water. You should have a pitcher right by your bed. Don't just sip one drop through a straw. Drink a lot, even if you don't feel like it. Remember that guy on the radio who talked about "dehydrated brains"? We laughed out loud, but there might be something to it. Drink two glasses in the morning before your breakfast tray comes. If you can get up, run the hot-water tap in the bathroom and drink from that. Warm water is better to drink in the morning than cold.

4) Around dinner time the nurse will give you a menu to check off what you want to eat for breakfast the next day. You *can* write in things that are not on the list. Because you aren't exercising, write in *dish of prunes*. Write in *100 percent whole-wheat toast*. They probably won't have that kind of bread, but it may shake them up a

bit. And by the next time one of us is in the hospital they might have it. Write in *Shredded Wheat* if you want it instead of cooked cereal, especially if the cooked cereal is creamy-white, pudding-like stuff. You can order two beverages: a glass of lowfat milk and a cup of decaffeinated coffee.

5) When the time comes to check off your lunch menu, cross out the soup because it will be salty. Write in *dish of raw carrot and celery sticks.* For dessert, cross out *pudding* and write in *half a grapefruit.* Or *orange.* Maybe *apple* too. You need three servings of fruit a day to keep from being constipated when you're flat on your back in bed. The fruit cup is all right, but fresh fruit is best. You will be tempted by apple pie or butterscotch chiffon tapioca, but desist. Resist too. You aren't climbing mountains.

6) For dinner write *salt-free* over your choice of meat or fish. Maybe the doctor ordered a salt-free diet for you and maybe he didn't. (Did you ask him to?) You can order two vegetables. Or write *dish of raw broccoli tips.* I wonder if they have raw broccoli. Maybe frozen is easier for hospitals to handle. For dessert write *fresh fruit—surprise me.* For beverage, order both lowfat milk and something hot. Maybe Postum. Or try an herb tea. Yes, write *herb tea* and see what comes.

7) You can refuse the sleeping pill. Tell the nurse you'd rather have a vitamin pill. Or a glass of milk and a graham cracker. (You may find out if the old story is true: "They wake you up to give you a sleeping pill.")

8) You can refuse pain pills. If you're not in pain, why take a pill? Say very politely to the nurse, "I'd rather not." For sure don't take both a sleeping pill and a pain pill.

9) If you can't sleep, walk around the hospital. Ask the doctor or the nurse and then go for a stroll. Nowadays they *want* you to be "up and at 'em." Even in South America they did. Remember how they put you out of the hospital the day after you had your appendix out? You're tough.

10) You'll feel terrible coming out of the anesthesia. You won't feel like eating, but force yourself to drink fruit juice anyway. Ask for both grapefruit juice and apricot nectar. As soon as you sip on those two glasses of fruit juice, you'll begin to feel better and then perhaps you can eat toast or a whole meal—a late lunch!

I also wrote on the bottom of the list: *You'll probably do none of these.*

He didn't. He was constipated.

How to Deal With the Dentist

"I know I'm wrong," I said to the dentist. "It's impossible, but I have this feeling. Every time I go to the dentist I have a cavity."

The dentist paid no attention.

I went on. "I feel it's like a Murphy's Law or something. One cavity each six months, but if I come only once a year I have one per year. And that time I got mad and came only once in three years I had only one cavity in three years."

No answer.

I went on. "Is it possible all that teeth cleaning is poking holes in my teeth? And why won't anyone tell me if my teeth really need cleaning? I have this picture of all these handsome young dental hygienists in beautiful green or blue smocks cleaning perfectly clean teeth while all over the world millions of horribly caked-on, plaque-plagued chompers are falling right out of people's heads. And not just in other countries either, but right next door to these beautiful, MUZAK-filled, padded, chrome-yellow Holiday Inn suites.

"It's like when the doctors were giving yearly physicals. Suddenly it came out that doctors were earning a fine living examining perfectly healthy individuals while the people who were sick were waiting in line at the NO INSURANCE? WAIT HERE window."

Still no answer from the dentist.

"Doctor, tell me. Do my teeth need cleaning?"

Dumb question. You can't get into that inner sanctum without going through the carwash first.

The dentist finally spoke. "I'm going to send you for X-rays."

I started in again. "That's another thing. I'm not happy about all the X-rays you've taken. We always find the cavities when you poke around and I say 'ouch.' "

"Excuse me," the dentist said. "I have another patient waiting."

Dear Dental Clinic,
We are at peace now. We have come to terms. I know I missed the fourth session of the flossing class, but when the receptionist called up and asked for "Kim" it sounded like "little Kim" and I said, "She's in kindergarten. I'll give her the message."

10 Ways To Be a Tooth Consumer

I don't mean that you're swallowing teeth. It's just the way we talk nowadays. We're all consumers.

Resolved: I will do my part so the dentist can do his.

1) I will brush and floss thoroughly every day.

2) I will not stick my teeth together with sugar.

3) I will consider honey as sugar when it comes to teeth.

4) I will consider dried fruit as sugar when it comes to teeth.

5) When I eat granola or gorp, I will finish my snack with the peanut part of the mixture. Peanuts help clean the sticky fruit or honey-coated cereal from teeth.

6) I will drink plain water instead of soda pop as much as possible. After I drink anything sweet, I will drink plain water to rinse my mouth.

7) I will chew instead of drinking. That is what teeth are for. He who washes his food down will find that teeth fall out from lack of exercise.

8) I will feed my teeth the same good food I feed my body.

9) I will not fall into the toothpaste trap. I will write down how much money I spend on toothpaste in one year. Then I will spend it on something else.

YOU GOT TO BE SMARTER THAN THEM. That is the law of advertising. They try to be smarter than you. You have to be smarter than them. (I know it should say *they* and not *them*, but this is like an advertising slogan.)

Fortunes are made on toothpaste. Why should you add to that when baking soda is right in your cupboard?

Mom, it's too late for my teeth, but you were right. I put a piece of paper in my typewriter and wrote that sentence to my mother. (In my family we don't telephone except when someone dies.) *Mom, you were so smart, and we kids wouldn't listen.*

It's true. Mom and Pop said use baking soda and salt, not toothpaste. We kids went to school, got a free sample of toothpaste (not unlike baby formula in the Third World) and we were spoiled. "Mom, it says right here don't use baking soda. It scratches the enamel on your teeth. We have to use toothpaste."

Buy toothpaste for seven children during the Great Depression? We didn't even buy milk. When the cow went dry, the milk supply went dry.

So did we kids go back to baking soda? Certainly not. The Great White Father of America had spoken. Pop and Mom were Hungarian immigrants. We kids were American. Americans used toothpaste. Or nothing.

Now it's OK to use baking soda—with salt and hydrogen peroxide. The three together will strengthen your gums and help prevent periodontal disease. Even many dentists will now tell you this. Here's the recipe:

BAKING SODA-SALT-&-HYDROGEN PEROXIDE
TEETH CLEANER
(Invented by Dr. Paul Keyes)
(International Dental Health Foundation, Reston, Virginia)

1 teaspoon 3% hydrogen peroxide
1/2 teaspoon baking soda
1/8 teaspoon table salt dissolved in 1/2 cup warm water
(If you're avoiding table salt, use Epsom salts instead.)
Pour the hydrogen peroxide into a bottle cap. Moisten the toothbrush in the hydrogen peroxide, then dip into baking soda. Apply mixture to teeth and gums, being careful to work it into gum margins. After brushing, rinse with the salt solution.

10) I will not ask for painkiller for a small cavity.

You can go for a dental checkup
and come out dead.
They'll inject you with Nisentil
and Phenargan and maybe add nitrous-oxide gas.
They love to work on bodies instead of
people. Bodies are so quiet. They give you
no trouble.
You can work in peace.
"Be nice now."

Don't be nice. Say NO.
You can stand a little pain.
Think of blue skies and the fact
that you'll walk out of the dentist's office
alive.

How to Keep From Acquiring a Basketful of Eyeglasses

"They come to me with a basketful of eyeglasses," the ophthalmologist said. I was talking to him during my appointment. We became quite friendly. I had already asked if I really needed new glasses. I hadn't changed them in 10 years, so you might think, "Lordy, what is this woman coming to? The same glasses for 10 years and she asks if it's necessary to change them now?"

Guess what the ophthalmologist said. "Actually no. There is a small change in your prescription, but as long as you're asking me, I shall tell you. You will not see much differently."

I was rather surprised. I mean—10 years with the same glasses, and now I'd probably go another 10—well, at least three.

That's when the ophthalmologist made the remark about people coming with a basketful of glasses. "Not one is comfortable," they say. "I need new glasses." They expect a miracle.

Actually I did too. I told myself, "When I get new glasses, my eyes will feel like new."

The doctor, now talking like a friend, said, "You will never be completely comfortable. You have a very strong prescription. And you have to change from far-vision glasses to reading glasses. Your eyes have to adjust one way and then back to another way, and the third way is when you go with no glasses at all."

Then the doctor used a rather surprising metaphor. "It's like using a new pair of shoes every day, or maybe two pairs. You get up, walk around with no glasses—your eyes work for you that way. Then you put on reading glasses and read the paper—OK, your eyes adjust to those lenses. Then you change to distance lenses and go outside. Your eyes adjust again. This goes on all day, back and forth."

And with me, one eye is much more nearsighted than the other. It's a wonder my eyes have done as well as they have all these years.

Actually they're in better shape now than they were 20 years ago. I can read all night if I want to. So here's my advice on

10 Ways to Avoid a Basketful of Eyeglasses

1) Keep a chart of your prescriptions. It's not against the law to copy the prescription before you give it to the optical shop. In fact, there will be times when you'll look at the chart and say, "Hey, this brand-new prescription is almost exactly the same as the one from three years ago. I'll call the oculist and ask him if I can use those glasses." Of course if your insurance or the government is paying for the new glasses—well, the temptation will be great.

2) Don't be shy about asking the optometrist or ophthalmologist (consult your dictionary for the difference between the two) the following question: "Is this change necessary? What dire catastrophe will happen if I stay with my present lenses?" You'll be surprised how often the answer will be, "Nothing will happen. You can do it." Of course if your eye doctor owns the eyeglass shop, there will be great crosscurrents at work. You might have to take that into account.

3) Don't expect new glasses to be your miracle. I wrote the following sentences to paste on my mirror: *I don't expect to see perfectly. I know there will be times my eyes are uncomfortable. It might have to do with my liver, or my stomach, or the sun, or the TV.*

4) Take that sun business seriously. I mean it. I know people who lie on their backs at the beach, practically staring at the sun, not even using the skimpiest of sunglasses because it would mar their "perfect tan."

5) Don't hock your house for new frames. If the optician says, "I'm afraid your frames will break if I try to put new lenses into them," say, "We're like Avis. We have to try harder."

6) Be wary of big frames. My ophthalmologist friend told me, "Large lenses may be beautiful and fashionable, but you can get distortion, especially in strong prescriptions." And face it, your nose may be too small to hold up large frames.

7) Don't buy tinted glasses without a good reason. Vanity is not a good reason. I know. I once had prescription sunglasses. I was so taken with them I wore them day and night. The minute I took them off I was winking and blinking like a mole. Luckily I broke them. Now I can see again. I am not tied to sunglasses like an umbilical cord anymore.

If your reason for wearing tinted glasses is "The lights in my office are too bright," stand up and holler about the lights. Don't creep off to the oculist. Who set the lighting standards for schools, libraries and public buildings? If you look into it, you will find that we used to let the fox guard the henhouse—the fox being the utility companies.

"You'll ruin your eyes with that dim light." I heard that all my life. Now I find out you don't ruin your eyes with dim light. It's too-bright light that can ruin your eyes.

This proves DOUBT EVERYTHING. I always say, "Wait a year or two. It'll come out that the exact opposite of what's being said now is the truth."

8) You can strengthen your eyes. Why don't I need sunglasses now? Why can I read all night? It might be the quantities of baked squash and raw, grated carrot I'm eating. It might be the 100-count bend and stretch I do every night. It might be my herb teas. Proper elimination is the secret to a great deal of good health, too. How about the elimination of my periodontal infection? And of course there's that "dim light I'm ruining my eyes with."

9) Don't pop your children into glasses as automatically as Christmas follows Thanksgiving. Anybody can have an off day while taking a test. Maybe the answer is a second test or more baked squash or less TV.

I once flunked the eye test for the Women's Army Corps (WAC). I did eye exercises for two months and improved my vision so much that I passed the test. By then I'd changed my mind, so I never joined. But the point is I could have.

10) You can buy reading glasses in the drugstore. Of course everyone will tell you, "They'll ruin your eyes!" They won't. Try them on—they're only magnifying glasses. If you can see with them, buy them. You can pay $150 to get the same thing from your eye doctor and see practically the same.

Doubt Everything

The reason I doubt everything—sometimes including what I say myself—is that for years I went around telling everyone I had a three-legged-stool approach to good health that worked. At least it did for me. But suddenly it came to me that I wasn't living by that formula at all. This is what it was:

1) Good food
2) Proper exercise
3) Peace of mind

Look at it. It's a perfect formula for being a lump.

You know perfectly well that you can stuff yourself with alfalfa sprouts and lowfat cottage cheese and still drop dead. You can hop and skip and bend and stretch and top it off with 10 miles a day cross-country and it won't get you to heaven.

As for peace of mind, which is now stress management, you can spend all of your days and nights cultivating the peace, managing the stress—

> How's your stress, my dear?
> Fine, thank you.
> You're still a lump.
> Give up smoking, my dear.
> Give up drinking, my dear.
> Give up eating, my dear.
> Doctor, my dear,
> you haven't told me
> WHAT THE HELL FOR!

Isn't this a law of physics (or is it chemistry?): If you leave a vacuum, something will fill it.

I nailed the following thesis to the door of the Senior Citizen Center:

> *Don't natter on with drug seminars.*
> *We know we have arthritis.*
> *Give us something bigger than arthritis.*
> *WE WISH TO BE INVOLVED, TO SEEK, TO QUEST,*
> *TO ADVENTURE, TO LAUGH AT DEATH.*
> *"LET IT COME! I HAVE LIVED!"*

Lucy, my pseudo-housekeeper in South America, who never cleaned the house but was my friend, confidant, mother and sister—and a poet—once said to me, "Why do you live in this big house and I don't have a house at all?" She also said to me: "Remember that movie we went to (it was *Sinbad the Sailor*) with that man who went all over and many things happened to him? Well, I think my life is like that. Many things have happened to me."

They did, Lucy. They did. You never did the housekeeping because you had to stand in the middle of the living room when I was trying to type a letter on my typewriter. "It was like this—" you would say, and I would have to take my letter out of the typewriter, put in a clean piece of paper and you would dictate.

♦ How you ran down a fox on your own two feet.

♦ How you swallowed strychnine and survived.

♦ How you helped your grandmother in the garden of the puma.

♦ How you worked for a woman with one eye and no nose who didn't pay you and you climbed a 10-foot-high fence in the middle of the night to escape.

"I still have adventures to live," you told me in your half-serious, half-*Que será, será* way. "I must own property. I must get married. Then I shall be a mother. But maybe not. I'll be a widow and then I will die."

Death came before you were a widow, Lucy, but you lived. You wrote a poem *To the Ant Who Didn't Know How to Pray.* You had a fight with the Catholic church. You went to political meetings. You joined a union. Lucy, you LIVED. You weren't a lump.

I was the lump. You were fighting. I had symptoms. In that country-club life we Americans were leading in Chile during the 1950s and 1960s, I had nothing better to do than have symptoms. Looking back on it I know I was homesick. I missed my job—which wasn't any job at all (assistant to an assistant in the advertising office of *Flower Grower* magazine in New York City)—but I still missed it.

I wasn't born into this castle-servant-walled-in-garden life, playing bridge, playing tennis, playing Lady Bountiful—playing, PLAY-ING.

I thought I had amoebas, tuberculosis, cancer, dysentery. I was tested for all of them. Poor doctors. I don't blame them at all. What could they do for me? One gave me cortisone pills. The second gave me hormone pills. I had to go to the library and get a dictionary in four languages to find out what kinds of pills they were. I was so young and dumb, I didn't know what hormones were and what they were supposed to do for me.

The third doctor—this one a woman German doctor—said to me, "Your hands are perspiring. I think you have nerves. I will give you something to calm them."

By pure accident I fell into a new world and I forgot my symptoms. It was a kind of job—not much of a job—teaching one class at a girls' school two blocks from our house, but suddenly I was in a whole new world. I had to study, correct papers, do projects, go to teachers' meetings.

Can you imagine? I loved those teachers' meetings. I never missed one. I went to pep rallies, flag day, graduation. Everything that went on at the school—I was there. I walked in the rose garden; I took tea; I belonged.

I wrote in my passport—*Occupation: Teacher.*

From this girls' school I went on to the university. The pedagogy school asked me to teach a class in English composition. "Good heavens," I said, "I can't teach at a university. I'm not even qualified to teach kindergarten."

"You need *more* qualifications for that," my friend Barbee, who also taught at the university, said. "You can do it."

So I did. In a run-down building at the other end of the city, carrying my own toilet paper, wearing gloves and a woolly hat because the doors didn't close and the windows didn't close, going on the bus for an hour and a half, coming home on the bus for an hour and a half.

"I'm like the Peace Corps, but I don't have the peace nor the corps," I said to my country-club friends.

Secretly I said to Lucy, "It's an adventure, an *AVENTURA.*" Mel was traveling. He was a mining engineer—that's why we were in South America. Lucy would wait up for me as I came home in the dark, my papers in a string bag, my legs ramrod-stiff from standing up and teaching four hours, then standing up an hour and a half on the bus.

"Oh Lucy," I would sigh. She would make a small dish of egg dumplings in chicken broth. We would sit by the fireplace, one on each side, plus the cat and the dog. Lucy would knit and I would eat my egg dumplings and recount the latest segment of the *AVENTURA.* It had to be told. Lucy's turn would be when she had her day off and went to a political meeting or to the union; or to visit her sister who had five children and an errant husband and lived in a slum; or to see her fat friend who worked for a rich Chilean family and had to bathe the "odd" aunt who lived in the attic.

Along with the university work, I started doing a column for the local English-language weekly. It wasn't a great paper, but they printed my column "Under the Lemon Tree." Mel's boss called it "Under the Bunion Tree." He was an Englishman and had that kind of wit.

When Mel and I left Chile, I brought exactly the same self to Montana. And whether by luck or accident (or did I SEEK AND QUEST?) I landed in practically the same kind of life—a little teaching, a little writing. But, it's not exactly the same.

Dear Dotty, I wrote to my Cornell University roommate who married a Chilean and has lived down there ever since, *We go to*

Causes up here. Down there it was cocktail parties. Here it's Causes.

I reached 62 this year. I wrote my epitaph. I do that every once in a while. It sort of sums up where you've been and where you're going. Once I was even paid for an epitaph—$5 from the *Portland Oregonian.* I wrote something like:

> *If you must give my soul to another,*
> *give it to one*
> *who sees the mountain breathe.*

This year I wasn't as poetic. I simply wrote:

> *I'm a small teacher,*
> *a small poet,*
> *a small writer,*
> *in a small city*
> *in Montana—*
> *and it's OK with me.*

I made a New Year's resolution: Just keep on trekking. Hold on to my head and my liver and my tendons so I can do at 72 more or less what I'm doing at 62.

> *I don't mind being dead*
> *but I don't want to be*
> *half dead.*

To the End of the Road and Beyond: My Husband

"Don't go, Mel," I said to my husband. "You've already used up your nine lives. One of these days your bones are going to be found on a mountain top."

Mel was packing his ice-fishing gear. He was going to fish through the ice at Georgetown Lake. He and two friends were going to leave at midnight, drive to the lake and fish until dawn on the theory—absolutely untested—that the Kokanee salmon bite only in the pre-dawn hours.

"It's 10 below zero now," I went on. "By midnight it will be 20 below. Or 30. On that windblown lake it'll be 50 below. Are you mad?"

"I've built a tepee," Mel said. "I'll sit inside."

"Mel, remember what happened last winter when you went snowshoeing at 10 below? You didn't get to the cabin, and you had to sleep under a bridge. At 74 years of age at 10 below zero to sleep under a bridge—is that sane? Is that sensible? To carry four kinds of heart medicine in a backpack and go snowshoeing at 10 below—is that sane? Is that sensible?"

"We expected to reach the cabin," Mel said.

Well, he did expect to, and he wasn't alone. He was with two companions. But they were 39 and 40. And they weren't taking heart medicine.

"You know that bridge," Mel said. "You've been there."

"Yes, in summer. You can hike 10 or 15 miles in summer but should you expect to do that on snowshoes in winter?"

"We didn't expect to. We expected to drive another four miles, but the road wasn't plowed out."

"Why didn't you turn around?"

"We thought about it."

But of course they didn't do it. To the end of the road and beyond: the credo of the mountaineers.

I'm truly surprised that Mel is still here. I'm sure he has literally used up his nine lives. He used up five in Ecuador where he went as a young, just-out-of-college mining engineer. Before I knew him, luckily, he. . .

1) . . .fell off a cliff with his horse Baldy. It took five Indians five hours to cut a trail to rescue the horse. Mel held the horse's head all that time.

2) . . .got scurvy. In the 20th century, living in Ecuador where oranges fall off the trees on your head, he got scurvy.

3) . . .had intestinal worms so bad he had to crawl to the doctor on his hands and knees. The cure was carbon tetrachloride, which was so drastic you couldn't even crawl on your hands and knees. It was on your stomach then.

4) . . .got an abcess on his kidneys. By the time he floated downriver to Guayaquil where there was a doctor, he was seeing yellow stars.

5) . . .had malaria twice. The first cure was quinine, which splits your head open and whips your stomach into a whirlpool. Atabrine was around by the second time, and that was fine. Mel looked like a plucked yellow chicken and he shook night and day, but he recovered faster. The quinine cure takes a month.

These are just the near disasters I *know* about. I didn't meet Mel until he was 40. You would think he'd be content to play chess now. I mentioned it to him. "I'll get you a chess set for Christmas."

"I'm too old to take up something like that," he answered.

"Look," I said as he packed two sandwiches and two thermoses, "If you come back with your fingers frozen and your toes frozen don't expect sympathy from me."

People hate people who say things like that. But sometimes you have to do it.

Not that it does a bit of good. The kind of people you say those things to will keep right on doing what they've been doing. In Mel's case, for 75 years.

The temperature on Georgetown Lake did go to 30 below and Mel did frost one finger. "I had to keep taking off my mittens to put a new maggot on the line," he explained.

But didn't I write *TO SEEK, TO QUEST, TO ADVENTURE?* Mel, I'll give you sympathy.

How Not to Cure
Lower Back Trouble

The doctor had Mel in traction. (This was while we were in South America.) Mel's back was giving him trouble. It was no wonder. Besides falling off a cliff on his horse in Ecuador, he'd fallen through a bridge fishing on the Argentine border. And then one New Year's Eve he caught a partying friend when she jumped into his arms.

"Rest," the doctor said. "Stay in bed. But get up from time to time and hang from the rafters."

The idea was to get the pressure off the vertebrae. It might have helped and it might not have. Mel got tired of rest, bed and hanging himself. "Let's go fishing at Lake Maule," he said.

"Are you mad?" I said.

We went anyway, driving along a goat trail to the top of a mountain, then hiking into a small lake beyond a large lake. The large lake was full of fish, but we were going to fish in the small lake. This is a logic completely understandable to fishermen.

Mel caught too many fish—not too many for the legal limit, as there wasn't any—but too many for carrying four miles back to the car. I already had the daypack with the equipment on my back. There was no help for it. Mel had to carry out the fish, four fish weighing five pounds each. Twenty pounds is a mere trifle for any hiker or backpacker, but Mel wasn't supposed to carry anything.

Did I say to him, "You'll ruin your back forever"? I hope I didn't. Of course I remember that I did.

Anyway, we arrived at the car, we drove home, we ate supper and we went to bed.

The next day Mel woke up, and his back was better than it had been in months. "I don't understand this," he said. I didn't either. We didn't dare consult with the doctor.

This wasn't a one-time freak happening. Mel has done this ever since. It's almost a joke with us. When his back starts bothering him one of us will say, "Time to go backpacking."

Does the friction wear away some deposit or something? We don't know. And certainly it wouldn't work for other people. I shudder to even think of anyone trying it.

Backpacking Energy Comes and Goes

How could I do a thing like that? As soon as I put the phone down I realized how foolish it was. A lady gave me 25 pounds of plums and I asked her if I could use her phone to call my husband to come in the car and pick me up.

I sat down under the plum tree and I thought to myself—why did I do that? I'm the same person who hiked up Stuart Peak with my backpack on my back. Yes, I finally took up backpacking. Well, what can you do when you're married to the Last of the Mountain Men, as our friend Ben Cave labeled Mel.

I was 55 when I buckled on that backpack frame for the first time. But I was never going to be any younger. If I was going to see the tops of the mountains, I'd have to do it now.

With 32 pounds on my back I climbed Stuart Peak, starting at 4000 feet altitude and ending at 8000 feet—all in one day, starting at 5 a.m. OH DEAR!

Mel and I climbed right up that mountain with our huge backpacks—tent, sleeping bags, stove, pots and pans, food, extra clothes—everything we needed to live three days in the wilderness.

I thought I was going to drop dead. I'd never hiked 12 miles in one day in my whole life—even without my bed and board on my back, loaded down like a pack mule. Of course that's exactly what you are when you backpack—your own pack mule.

Well, I made it up the mountain, but I was positive I'd never make it down again. I thought I'd wake up in the morning stiff as a board. My ankles wouldn't work. My back would be bent into a V and would never straighten out. How would I get down the mountain? They'd have to send a helicopter up after me.

The truth is I woke up perfectly all right. Mel and I climbed another peak in the area, then went down to a lake and spent the night on the shore. We ate fish for supper—after we caught a second batch. The first batch we left for just five minutes and Pffsst! they were gone. A hawk or raven must have swooped down and carried them off right behind our backs.

Actually I was supposed to be watching the fish, but I was inside the tent trying to escape the wildlife. Mosquitoes, gnats and horse-flies were in clouds. I swallowed two mosquitoes right along with the fish. But I didn't die of that either.

The third day we climbed up the ridge from the lake, then hiked down the mountain, 12 miles.

I was amazed. I never thought I had that much strength. I actually didn't think I could hike 12 miles with 32 pounds on my back. Later I said to my health class at the university, "If I have all this strength that I didn't know I had, well, how about everyone else? Do we all have tremendous strength and energy that we're not using?"

I guess so because I did three more backpacks that summer. I felt strong as a horse, sleek as a greyhound. (Not really. I lost five pounds, then gained them right back.) But I was proud of myself—at 55, going on 56, spending the summer backpacking. HALLE-LUJAH!

So then, why did I sit under a plum tree looking at a small sack of plums and call for my husband to come and get me in the car? Is there a direct ratio between how far you are from home and how much strength you have?

When Mel arrived I said to him, "This is awful. Next shopping day we're going to put our backpacks on our back and walk to the market."

"You can do that," Mel said. "I'll meet you there."

Eunice Brown,
What's Your Secret?

"How are you, Kim Williams?" my neighbor said. This is my 89-year-old neighbor, Eunice Brown, speaking.

"Well, actually—" I started.

"Don't tell me," Eunice said.

I stopped and stared. Eunice laughed. "I'll make a bargain with you," she said. "You don't tell me how you are, and I won't tell you how I am."

I had to laugh, of course. If I told her all the details of the ankle I had recently twisted and the cut on my finger, and then she told me all of her details. . . I know she has arthritis and she's hard of hearing and her back bothers her. But if we went through all that, we would never get to the roses in her yard and the iris show coming up, and the visit from her sister.

Actually Eunice should have told me how she was because she was just out of the hospital. Maybe she shouldn't have been out at all. She was in an automobile accident just the day before. The car rolled on "black ice." Neither Eunice nor the driver was hurt badly, but they were taken to the hospital for a checkup.

"I signed myself out," Eunice said.

"Eunice," I said, "you're black and blue, and you're 89 years old. You can't go to that party tonight even if it is for the handicapped children and you bought two tickets for $100."

"They expect me to be there. I've got my ribs strapped and I'll take two aspirin. Do you want to see my dress?"

"Not your Indian costume!"

"No. I'm going in lace. With a big hat. And red shoes."

Eunice could go as anything. Her house is so full of clothes, antiques, bric-a-brac and plain junk that she could open a store. In a way she does have a store. At 89 she deals—buys and sells.

"Her mind is sharp as a trap," her competitors say.

But don't the doctors say, "Use it or lose it"? Eunice uses it—it being everything: body, soul, brain, spirit.

One of these days Eunice is going to fall apart like the one-horse shay. All of us along the block say this. We've been saying it for 10 years. We'll probably be saying it for another 10.

We watch her little white car flying in and out of her driveway, day and night, seven days a week. She goes to breakfast; she goes to lunch; she goes to dinner. Not alone. Never alone. Eunice lives in people. She takes them out; they take her out. They give parties; she gives parties. At 89 she can give a luncheon for 30 people. Home-cooked, starting with whole, fresh chickens from the butcher.

I invited Eunice to talk to my health class at the university. Did I pick her up and take her? No. She picked me up and took me. "I'm going to teach you to drive, Kim Williams," she said.

She would too. Eunice believes in one-on-one doings. She was in a disagreement with her church not long ago. She came over to my house one midnight—she and I visit at midnight when we see each other's lights on—and announced, "I was almost thrown out of my church."

"Why?" I asked.

"Oh, not really," she said, "but I had to explain why I spoke up. It was on account of collecting money for missionary work in the South Seas. I said that I was not going to give money for any more missionary work in the South Seas or any place for that matter outside of the United States."

"You don't believe in missionary work?" I asked.

"That's the easy way out," Eunice said. "Write a check, put on the bottom—for missionary work—and put it in a basket." I don't think that makes us understand anything. Right here in Missoula I know three families who would like to come to church but they don't know how to start. They feel that they don't know anyone. They don't have the right clothes. And they don't know if anyone would welcome them. Now, that's the kind of missionary work I can understand. Take one family at a time, call on them, say 'May I come in my car and take you to church on Sunday?' Take the mother out to lunch. Maybe no one has ever taken that woman to lunch in a nice place in her whole life. After lunch you say to her, 'See that blouse in that window? It is made for you.' You go into the store with the woman, she tries on the blouse, you buy it for her, and you do it nicely so she can accept it."

"Most of us don't know how to do things that way," I said.

"I'm 89 years old," Eunice said. "Nobody gets mad at me."

Eunice, I wish you had known my Lucy. Not to do missionary work for—or to. Not at all. I see you and Lucy sitting side by side exchanging stories. "It was like this. . ." Lucy said. You do the same, Eunice. You dine out on stories. People go around saying, "If you haven't heard Eunice Brown's story about the fish-egg breakfast, you haven't lived."

And your costumes, Eunice. You dress up. You make it easy for people to have a good time. To laugh. You came over one midnight to show me your antique costume. "When I go to an antique show," you said, "I dress like an antique."

Did someone from on high write on your forehead, Eunice— "Thou shalt uplift thy fellow man"?

It's valid, you know. Even doctors are saying it now—this business of laughing and helping other people laugh is as valid as using aspirin or taking out an appendix when it's infected.

Norman Cousins made a tremendous impression on the medical establishment when he wrote about his recovery from a very serious illness. He said that laughing definitely helped.

I went to an educational conference the first week Mel and I moved back from South America. Imagine—I'd been in Missoula one week, I read in the paper *Educational Conference at Sentinel High School,* and I was so accustomed to going to teachers' meetings that like Pavlov's dog, I salivated and went.

It was worth it. A Dr. William Glasser was brought to Missoula to speak and he said something that struck a gong in my brain. "Teachers," he said, "it is your duty to make your students laugh once a day."

Glory be! So I was doing right in Chile. When I taught at the university and all the students looked aghast when I spoke Spanish because my accent was so bad, I said, "That's all right—my accent in English isn't very good either." Then we all laughed and went on from there.

Eunice, I love your costumes. I love your stories. Thank you.

How To Prevent Colds

What's the magic formula for not having colds? This question came on a postcard from George Smith of White Salmon, Washington.

I think there is a little magic connected with not having colds. But I do have a formula of sorts. It seems to work for my husband and me. Neither of us has many colds.

10 Ways to Prevent Colds

1) First of all, eat real food—none of that pre-cooked, pre-digested, two-minute, three-minute stuff. So much has been done to that food you might as well eat sawdust and melt a vitamin pill on top. I know you don't have time to cook, and nobody will eat your cooking, and who wants to be a slave to the kitchen. I don't spend a lot of time cooking myself. And Mel doesn't do it either. You can cook real food and not take a lot of time. See page 69.

2) Eat enough food to keep your resistance up. I don't think you can live on vitamin pills, protein drinks and diet pop and keep your resistance up. You need real food and quite a lot of it. Oh ho! Then of course you have to exercise or you'll get fat.

3) I believe in the kind of exercise where you huff and puff. It has a fancy name—aerobic or something similar. Anyway, you have to work up a sweat. You can wash down the walls of your kitchen if you wish.

4) Keep your guts warm. "Your daughter is going to get a liver chill," I said to Trixie one day. Of course Trixie hooted and hollered.

Everyone knows teenagers can wear mini-skirts in a blizzard. That may be so but I lived in South America for 18 years, in the shadow of the Andes Mountains, and everyone there knew what a liver chill was. When your liver got cold, your whole digestive system went on the blink. I sometimes think what we call intestinal flu up here might be just a good old South American liver chill. Have you seen people changing a tire in midwinter? Their sweater slides up, their pants slide down, and a cold wind from Alaska hits their middle.

5) Wear a hat.
I am a babushka.
I wear a kerchief on my head,
winter and summer.
Do not laugh at me.
My mother did this
and she is here at 96.

I know—"Did you just get off the boat?" That's the picture. An immigrant woman with a kerchief tied under her chin. I'm turning into my mother.

I don't mind. Our house is at 65 degrees. I like that kerchief on my head.

Of course, outside I wear a woolly hat. On really cold days I wrap a scarf around my face so I breathe through the scarf and warm up the Arctic air.

6) Don't sit in a draft. You can run in a draft, walk in a draft, but you can't sit in a draft. I know this isn't scientific—doctors will pooh-pooh it, but there it is anyway.

Doctors also say people average six colds a year. Well, I don't believe that. I mean I don't believe that six colds are necessary.

7) Sleep with a window open summer and winter. Wear a nightcap like Scrooge in the *Christmas Carol.*

8) Get enough sleep to keep your resistance up. This may be five hours a night. It may be 10.

9) Don't sit and knit. The germs will descend upon you. You have to keep the adrenaline flowing:

Go

Be

Become.

10) Now we come to the bottom line, and here is the magic of the formula. It's as if someone casually asked you the question, "How are things with you?" How would you answer? Upbeat or downbeat? Remember in *Guys and Dolls* the girlfriend who kept sneezing? Her song was something like—"When a guy won't marry a girl, that girl is liable to come down with a cold." Well, that's the mystery.

Of course there was Frankie and Johnny, too. I don't picture Frankie as sneezing. I don't think she even carried a handkerchief.

How To Cure Colds

The letter was left in the typing room at the university. It was half finished and then discarded. It caught my eye because—well, the truth is I am a nosy person. I have to know everything. But the letter was worth reading. Here it is:

Howdy. (That's really how it started.)

Am I ever miserable. I've been able to dodge a cold for the last nine months, but now one has got a hold of me. It's one of those nasty head colds. What's worse, I'm high on the drugs that people have been giving me to fight the cold. Antibiotics, antihistamines, Tylenol, aspirin, Veramycin, decongestants, Vicks VapoRub—just name it and I've had it the last 36 hours. I really feel like just staying in bed, but you know you can't do that when things have to be done. Well, the long weekend is coming up, and everybody in the house is splitting for Grand Targhee and Jackson Hole for some skiing. I had a place in a car going south, but I had to back out.

You can see the picture. This poor student couldn't go on vacation with his friends because he had a cold. Almost worse than that, his friends were turning him into a walking drugstore. Well, you might say, what can a person do to cure a cold? Here's what I recommend:

10 Ways to Cure Colds

1) Buy a chicken. Hot chicken soup *does* help a cold. If you want to be technical you can say the soup "alleviates the symptoms." If you want to be non-technical—well, it just makes you feel better.

I like my chicken soup hot in two ways: hot from the stove and hot from chili pepper or cayenne.

2) Lock up the coffee, soda pop and drugstore remedies. They have caffeine in them. You feel better because you're being stimulated. You can keep going, but you might keep going too long. Without the stimulation your body will say, "Hey, lay off. I've had it."

3) Go to bed. The earlier you go to bed with your cold the quicker it will go away. In fact, some people nip the cold in the bud, so to speak.

4) Find an old, worn-out pair of flannel pajamas. When you have a cold, you need all the soft, squashy comfort you can get.

5) Sweat it out. I'm a firm believer in the sweat-it-out theory, but you have to do it right. You can't run to a sauna, sweat for 15 minutes, then go to the office and work 10 hours. You have to sweat it out at home in your own bed. The object is to raise your body temperature so it will kill the viruses (yes, I do know that colds are caused by viruses and not germs) in your system.

This is where you use the hot-soup regimen. Garlic soup is excellent. It is the same chicken soup mentioned earlier, but in addition to the chicken and hot pepper you add a fistful of raw, chopped garlic.

Then pile on the blankets, put socks on your feet, an undershirt under the flannel pajamas, wrap an old stocking around your throat, put your nightcap on, lie there and let the warmth permeate your bones.

6) Feed both the cold and the fever. I don't think your body can fight a cold without ammunition. It needs good food. Put whole-grain rice in the chicken soup. Add a carrot, a chunk of Hubbard squash, maybe even an egg if you have a real egg, one from a chicken that walked around on solid ground and ate bugs.

7) Add yogurt to your diet. The bacteria in the yogurt are "good" bacteria. They'll help fight the invading "bad" bacteria, germs, viruses—whatever.

8) Add fresh fruit and vegetables, lemonade and herb tea to your

diet. You don't want a clogged-up system. Constipation on top of a cold is awful. You want lots of fresh vitamins and good tastes. Make a big fruit salad.

9) Enjoy your misery. Wallow in it. Read nothing but junky books. Turn on the worst TV programs. Let your nose drip. Don't get up and dash off to the office or school until your strength has returned. It might take 24 hours, maybe 48, maybe 72.

10) Don't go past the reset point. Here is where your good judgment will come in. If you wallow in bed too long, instead of getting stronger, you get weaker. It's like riding the crest of the wave. You have to fling yourself out of bed and into life. It's time to GO and DO.

Is Herb Medicine Foolproof?

We were at a church supper and a friend said to me, "What's this red stuff in your potato salad?"

"That's bits of rose hips," I said.

"Huh," the friend said, "tell me—will rose hips really prevent a cold?"

"If you have faith," I said.

I was sort of kidding, but I really do believe that. How else can one explain herb remedies and folk medicine? Well, actually, how can one explain drugstore medicine? "Did it work?" the doctor asks.

I tell my health-food students, "We are all individual bundles of chemistry. What works for one person won't work for everyone."

A few years ago I burned my arm with boiling apple juice. It hurt so much I had to keep the arm in a pan of ice-cold water for three hours.

I had a jar of aloe vera gel, and I also had a big aloe vera plant growing on my window sill. I'd heard a lot about this plant so I decided to try it. I used both the fresh leaves and the bottled gel.

I was completely happy with the results. My arm didn't blister. It hurt, yes, and it was red as fire, but it healed without a scar.

Of course I had to endure scathing remarks from my friends:

"Stupid! Why didn't you go to the emergency room at the hospital?"

"What? You haven't been to the doctor yet?"

"At least go to the drugstore and ask the pharmacist for a salve."

"Are you a masochist?"

Will Kerling, my ex-fireman friend (I seem to have a great many ex-something friends) had a very deep burn on his neck from fighting a fire. A red-hot coal fell down his neck. He was getting drugstore medicines of all kinds, paid for by the insurance, but what really healed the burn, according to Will, was plain vitamin E. He opened capsules of liquid vitamin E and put the oil on his neck. "My neck felt good immediately," he said, "and it healed perfectly." He grinned. "I had to pay for the vitamin E myself."

Other people say the first thing to do for a burn is to swallow 1,000 milligrams of vitamin C. For the shock.

I'm not advocating any of these remedies. They'll work for some people. They won't work for everyone.

My students ask me, "Can you prevent hay fever by eating local honey and drinking tea made from local herbs?" I have to answer, "It might prevent your hay fever. It might also give you hay fever."

Herb medicine sounds simple. It isn't. When I went to an herb-medicine conference given by an Indian medicine man, his presentation shook up all my ideas.

"I like to have the patient stay with me for a few days," the medicine man said. "I want to feel what he feels. I listen to him, not just his words, but the talk of his body. Then I make a trip to the mountains and gather the herbs I want. I do not gather more than I need. I do not want to hurt the plant because how can the plant heal a suffering person if it is not in agreement with what I am trying to do? I pray with the plant, and then I pick it."

I talked this idea over with an Indian student here at the university. Michael and I have gone on plant walks together. "It's true," Michael said. "We Indians believe that healing through herb medicine involves a lot more than just the medicinal effect of the plant. When the medicine man gathers the herb himself there is a ceremony between him and the plant."

Maybe you could think of it as a dialogue. The medicine man takes the life of the plant, so he has to have an understanding with the plant. This is very important—that you are using the life of a plant to aid the life of a person. The medicine man feels this and passes on this feeling when he treats the patient.

"Glory be!" I said. "It's the laying on of hands." Or the spirit.

Food & Diet

I am not a fanatic about food.
Health food, junk food, gourmet food—
don't let it rule your life.
Food is fun: always ask for yuca
in the Amazon Jungle.
Food is fuel: stoke your engines,
gentlemen, and let's get on
with living.
Food is political: you are
what you eat; you are also
what eats you.

Eating bean sprouts will not save your soul.

The We-Keep-Waiting-For-Him-To-Drop-Dead Phenomenon

Every time I teach my good-nutrition class, a student will stand up in the first 10 minutes and say, "What about my grandpa who lived to be 89 and smoked two packs of cigarettes a day and drank whiskey to the day he died?"

Another student will say, "My grandmother lives on candy and cookies and ice cream and she mows her own lawn at 82."

We all know the story about the two sisters. One was a health nut, the other a junk-food addict. Who lived a long, hale and hearty life? Who succumbed to a fatal ailment at 52?

There's no rhyme or reason to this. I call it the *We-Keep-Waiting-For-Him-To-Drop-Dead Phenomenon.* There are people whose genes are marvelous. They have the constitution of a horse. They will live to be 100 unless they are hit by a two-ton truck.

But can you and I depend on that? Not always. For example, my sister and brother-in-law, Froni and Ken, drove to the Grand Canyon for vacation. Instead of seeing the Grand Canyon, they saw the inside of a hospital. They thought Ken had a heart attack. It was indigestion.

"You know how marvelous those cafe breakfasts are," Froni said. "Bacon, eggs, hashed browns, toast dripping with butter, coffee before you even sit down. We never eat like that at home. Then hamburgers and French fries for lunch. A steak for dinner. Well, we were on vacation."

I was on a candy-cake-ice cream-white bread-fried chicken routine once. I didn't land in the hospital, but I was as fat as a butterball. I weighed 160 pounds.

I feel much better on my present, more-or-less-health-food diet, and I can maintain a more-or-less normal weight.

My 10 Magic Foods

Dean and Judy had a creole ham dish ready for Mel and me when we arrived in New Orleans. After eating it, I promptly threw up.

"Tea and an aspirin?" Judy suggested. "Or bed?"

Mel and I had just arrived from 18 years in South America. Bag and baggage back to the USA. We had sold or given away 18 years of accumulation including house, car, dog and cat. We changed money on the black market. We lost money.

My stomach was in an uproar. I thought I had—no, I knew I had—the beginning of an ulcer. On the airplane coming from Santiago to Miami I kept asking for milk. "Please, more milk." The stewardess thought I was a lactating mother.

I got to New Orleans barely alive. I tried to eat the beans and ham creole, but I couldn't.

I went to bed, but I couldn't sleep. I needed food, but what could I keep down?

"Do you have a can of corn?" I asked Judy.

"Corn?" she repeated. She looked at me as if I'd asked for poison. "I think I could eat some canned corn," I said. "Whole kernel." Judy opened a can of corn and put two tablespoons in a pan. "More," I said.

I ate the whole can. Slowly. My stomach was in tatters. But it settled, so I went to bed and slept.

This has happened many times. Corn settles my stomach. It's one of my magic foods. I should carry a can like Linus carries his blanket.

I think everyone has 10 magic foods. Listen to your body, I say to my students. Then make your own list. Of course if you're smoking like a chimney, drinking like a fish, shooting up and coming down, I don't know what your body would say. Maybe just "Alas. . ." But normally you can count on your body craving the right thing. When you feel bad, instead of reaching for Maalox or Rolaids, reach for your list of magic foods. Didn't Hippocrates back in 500 B.C. say, "Let your food be your medicine?"

Kim Williams' 10 Magic Foods

1) Corn
2) Celery
3) Grapes
4) Yogurt
5) Apple
6) Lemon
7) Nanking cherries
8) Dandelion greens
9) Oatmeal
10) Yuca

These foods fix me up. When I had hepatitis in South America and the doctor put me on a 100% sugar diet (They did that in those days. I craved solid food but got angel-food cake and colored gelatin.), celery and grapes kept me sane.

Yogurt puts good bugs into my digestive system, and it's milk in a form much easier to digest than sweet milk. It tastes good too.

I use plain yogurt (we make it ourselves), not the kind with jam in it. I consider yogurt with fruit conserve in it a dessert. Plain yogurt is a main-dish kind of food. It's the difference between sweet and savory, as my British friends always pointed out when we were having tea. They meant did you want a sandwich or did you want dessert? The beauty is they gave you a choice. I hate gatherings where you have to load up on sugar or go hungry.

An apple a day is ancient, but still good:

An apple a day
sends pectin your way.

And pectin is good for the digestive system. I hope you can find good tart apples and not those market-savvy, hard-as-a-rock, but tasteless things you find in supermarkets. I doubt they help your digestion at all.

I learned the value of lemons in South America. My housekeeper Lucy squeezed lemon juice on everything—fish, meat, chicken, vegetables, salads—even the soft-boiled egg she ate for breakfast.

"What's that for?" I asked when I first saw the egg routine. "My stomach likes it," Lucy said.

Well, you can't argue with that.

Now I look back and I see that Lucy was very smart. Acid with an egg helps iron absorption and also the digestion of the protein, fat and cholesterol.

The lemons we ate in Chile were tree ripened. We picked the biggest, fattest, yellowest ones right from the tree in our garden. I could drink a lemonade without adding sugar.

I learned about Nanking cherries as a digestive aid here in Montana. People plant these ornamental shrubs as hedges. The small sour cherries are not in great demand so I can easily glean two gallons every summer. I freeze the fruit whole and there's my mid-winter tonic—a handful a day, like a magic talisman. (I said, didn't I, that each person must find his/her own 10 magic foods? Mine might sound very c ld to you.)

Dandelion greens are my spring tonic. I can't start the year without a dandelion salad. You could call it a ritual. Well, we need rituals.

About oatmeal: There's nothing as soothing as a bowl of creamy oatmeal when you're feeling low. I use old-fashioned rolled oats. That three-minute stuff is only good for wallpaper paste. No wonder whole generations of young people have turned off hot cereal.

Crazy, you'll say, but yuca is absolutely what you need in the tropics. Yuca is manioc root, and it's a staple of the natives. I always eat the native food when I'm in another country. In the Amazon—we were in Iquitos—the hotel tried to serve us steak and French fries.

"Bring me yuca," I said, "and fried bananas, black beans and rice."

"That's kitchen food," the waiter said.

"Fine," I said. "That's what I want."

You always have digestive upsets in the tropics. I love fruit and have to try it all. Well, yuca counteracts that indulgence. Besides, eating yuca or *feijoada* (the Brazilian national dish of black beans and rice and very odd parts of the pig) or *erizos* (sea urchins) is part of the traveling. It's an adventure. It's fun.

Why I Eat the Way I Do: 10 Helpful Hints

1) Don't DO So Much To the Food

I was making a list of foods for a friend who wrote to me about fingernails. "Mine are a mess," she said. "I know yours grow like mad. I remember you sitting on the floor at the gym cutting your nails with a toenail clipper. That's terrible. I hope you're not doing it any more."

I regret to say that I still clip my nails like a truck driver sitting on his runningboard. But it's true—they grow like mad.

So I wrote to Sharon and told her what I ate. I put the carbon copy of the letter into my file labeled *CURES*. I know very well that nothing *cures* anything, but some people are helped once in a while.

In the file I also came upon the carbon copy of a letter I once sent to a lady who wrote about thinning hair. "I'm getting bald," she wrote. "Any advice?"

My answer was: "I don't know anything about hair. I think a lot of it has to do with genes. But I have a plentiful mop, so if it has anything to do with what I eat, you are welcome to my diet."

I looked at the list of foods. My Lord, it was the same list I made for fingernails. Maybe I'd give the same list for arthritis if someone asked me. No, I wouldn't. I don't know anything about arthritis. All I can say is, "This is the way I eat, and this is the way I am after eating the way I do."

I think the common denominator of all my diets is to eat food that has had as little done to it as possible. I tell my students to eat food as close as possible to . . .

a) . . . the hole in the ground it came out of, or

b) . . . the limb of the tree it came off of.

2) Wheat Is Neat If Freshly Ground

Mel and I visited a ranch once. The owner ran some wheat through her new grinder. "Here's some real breakfast cereal," she said. "Cook it tomorrow morning."

That freshly ground wheat cooked up into a cereal that tasted as different as night and day from store-packaged cereal. No wonder Mel's fishing buddy, Larry, said, "I have eight kinds of cereal in my cupboard. I want to eat hot cereal for breakfast, but not one tastes like anything."

Larry, try some of this freshly ground wheat. Cook it up; smell it. You won't need to smother it with sugar or maple syrup or honey. Just add some real milk—you do need whole milk for cereal—and eat. The taste comes from the whole wheat, freshly ground.

Bread made from freshly ground flour is just like that cereal. It has a taste so good you don't even need butter. That's the kind of bread you can call the *staff of life*. It has all the vitamins and minerals of the grain seed that would be put into the ground to grow a new plant.

This kind of bread won't fatten you because it doesn't need to be dripping with butter or plastered with jam.

3) Salad Bars, I Love You

The salad bar is one of the greatest inventions of the century. A veggie, granola type can go out to eat right along with a red-meat freak and there's no hassle. Mel and I do exactly that. I order the salad bar. Mel has prime rib. I eat a bite or two of his meat if I wish.

I'm not a vegetarian, but I don't eat much meat. Actually, Mel doesn't either. We used to. I don't know why. I think it was just custom. That's what people did. I can remember being taken out to dinner by Mel's boss in South America and eating half a lobster and a huge steak at the same meal. Now I don't even want to look at people doing that.

I actually owned a French-fry kettle at one time. We made hamburgers and French fries for lunch at home. Now our lunch— each one makes his own—is a bowl of salad.

4) Eat It Raw

I'm not saying that raw food will grow hair in the middle of your bald head or cure your arthritis. I know, Melissa Kwasny, you sent me a clipping, "News From Basin," in which you interviewed a Mr. Homer Hughes, Sr., who said he cured himself of arthritis:

This is what I done and got rid of my aches and pains. Don't cook food. No booze, coffee, tea, milk, vinegar or white sugar. No pastries, pork, very little salt or flour.

How many people are paying $400 per week at a fat farm to find out exactly what Mr. Hughes put into the Basin, Montana, newspaper?

I think a great part of the magic of raw food is that—to use plain words—it's laxative. I bet that's what fat farms make millions on.

Certainly the laxative effect is a good part of the secret of old-time spring tonics. Eat a dandelion salad, the old recipe books said. Eat a "mess" of greens. Well, what does a grizzly bear do when he comes out of his den in early spring? He eats the first greens of spring. If the greens aren't up, he digs juicy, bitter roots.

5) Stir-fry Your Dinner

Stir-fry is another invention of the century. It's as old as the hills in other parts of the world, but it takes time for us bull-headed Americans to adopt ideas from the second, third and other worlds.

Stir-frying is as close as you can come to eating food raw without actually eating it raw and cold. It's like steaming, but you add a little oil or butter. You have all the flavor of the food. You don't need thick cream sauces.

Do you remember eating in fancy restaurants and being faced with the Great Problem of choosing a SAUCE? I mean, you had to KNOW HOW to choose a sauce. Mel and I were in Lyon, France, when he was in his Company phase. The local representative took us out to dinner. "No sauce, please," I said to the waiter. Probably it was the maitre d' or headwaiter. There were several chains of command.

"But, madam . . ." the waiter said.

"A good steak doesn't need any sauce," I said.

"Please . . ." our host interrupted. "You are in Lyon, France. This restaurant is famous for French cooking. The sauce is everything." I gave up. "OK, sauce." I hated it. I like the taste of basic, close-to-the-earth food. I don't need dressing on fruit salad. I don't need mayonnaise on cottage cheese. How often when you eat out do you get half a ladle of salad and a whole ladle of dressing?

6) Cook Ahead

The secret of my quick, healthy meals is to use the refrigerator for what it's meant for—to prepare food ahead. I always have a pot of cooked beans in the refrigerator. Not baked beans sticky with sugar. I have plain pinto beans cooked with oregano, sage and savory. Or I have garbanzo beans, also called chick peas, cooked with a bay leaf and basil.

I also have a pot of cooked brown rice, or a pot of bulgur wheat. My husband loves lima beans. We both like split peas. These can be the base for two or three meals. Lima beans with corn. Split pea soup with slices of cheese or hard-boiled egg. If you have a source of additive-free hot dogs, serve them with the lima beans.

I think we should fight for good hot dogs. Why should we give up a very handy food just because it's being overloaded with chemicals? Hot dogs and sausages can be made with herbs and spices instead of sugar and nitrites. They don't have to keep forever.

Stir-fry meals can be put together in 20 minutes if the brown rice is cooked ahead and has only to be reheated.

A roast chicken on Sunday means you have slivers of meat to add to the Tuesday stir-fry.

7) Choose Green and Yellow

I use lots of green and yellow vegetables because I believe that vitamin A works together with vitamin C in preventing colds. Also, I have the feeling my constant supply of baked winter squash helps my eyes.

8) Sprouts, Of Course

Sprouts are so "in" nowadays that the only new thing about them is that backpackers now sprout as they walk up and down mountains.

They keep little containers in their knapsacks.

9) Question Orange Juice

I eat grapefruit and oranges instead of drinking orange juice. My stomach, like Lucy's, has likes and dislikes. I know frozen orange juice—the great O.J.—is like mom and apple pie, but I think the companies are putting peel in it or something. My stomach tells me to eat the orange—or better yet—half a grapefruit.

10) Nonfat Powdered Milk: No Cholesterol, Plenty of Calcium

I am accustomed to a hot drink with milk in it. In South America you put a pot of hot milk on the table and people added coffee or tea. I say have a boiling teakettle and a jar of instant powdered milk. Some people will add instant coffee. Others will add chicory or Postum or blackstrap molasses.

Of all the sweetening agents, blackstrap molasses is the only one that adds anything really noticeable, nutritionally speaking, to your diet. Blackstrap molasses is rich in iron.

Most of all, I say KEEP IT SIMPLE. DON'T TORTURE THE FOOD. Those breakfast cereals that have been steamed and baked and puffed and crunched—how can food like that do you any good?

Maybe you have to re-educate your palate. DO IT.

10 Quick, Healthful Meals

(Directions are included for starred (*) recipes)

Day 1

Breakfast
1/2 grapefruit
Scrambled eggs with corn (canned is quickest)
Whole-wheat toast (barely buttered)
Hot milk flavored with blackstrap molasses

Lunch (brown bag)
Chunk of cold, baked sweet potato (Crazy? Try it.)
Yogurt ambrosia (plain yogurt with added grapes, canned peaches
and sunflower seeds)
2% milk
Herb tea or miso soup (Miso soup is available in health food stores in
individual packets. Stir into hot water. Look for low-salt miso.)

Dinner
Broccoli and chicken stir-fry*
Steamed brown rice
Fresh fruit
2% milk
Herb tea or hot lemonade

Broccoli and Chicken Stir-Fry
1 tablespoon oil
1 medium-size onion, cut in thin slices
1 small bunch broccoli, cut in bite-size pieces
1/2 cup raw carrot slices
1 cup cooked chicken, cut in small pieces
1/4 pound mushrooms, sliced
Dash of garlic powder
1 tablespoon soy sauce
1 tablespoon lemon juice

Heat oil in wok or heavy skillet. Stir-fry onion 3 minutes. Add broccoli and carrot. Stir-fry 5 minutes. Add all other ingredients. Stir-fry about 3 minutes more. (Serves 4)

Day 2

Breakfast
Whole orange
Rice patty*
Hot milk flavored with instant coffee, chicory, blackstrap molasses or a roasted-grain herb tea

Rice Patty
1 teaspoon oil
1 cup cooked brown rice
1 tablespoon water
1 ounce cheese, cut in thin slices
Place oil in skillet. Add rice and water. Cover and heat through. Lay cheese on top. Replace cover. Turn off heat and let skillet sit until cheese melts. (Serves 2)

Lunch (brown bag)
High-protein lunch salad (garbanzo beans, cottage cheese, banana, apricot and alfalfa sprouts)
Whole-wheat crackers (You can bake your own. There is a recipe in the book *Laurel's Kitchen.*)
2% milk
Herb tea

Dinner
Baked dinner (fish fillets in casserole dish with a squeeze of lemon juice on top; baked potato; baked Hubbard squash without the brown sugar. Start the potatoes and squash 30 minutes ahead of the fish.)
Watercress salad
Raw fruit
2% milk
Herb tea or hot lemonade

Day 3

Breakfast
1/2 grapefruit
Hot cereal with milk, sliced banana and a tablespoon of peanut butter
Hot milk flavored with blackstrap molasses

Lunch (brown bag)
Lima bean soup in thermos
Raw vegetables and hard-boiled egg
Fresh fruit
2% milk
Herb tea

Dinner
Rice-corn-tomato-cheese casserole*
Spinach salad
Fresh fruit
2% milk
Herb tea (or go ahead—splurge. Have real coffee. Have a piece of baked cheesecake to celebrate a friend's birthday.)

Rice-Corn-Tomato-Cheese Casserole
(I first ate this at an Ananda Marga Yoga house)
1 tablespoon oil
2 cups cooked brown rice
2 cups canned corn
2 cups stewed tomatoes (canned will do)
1/2 cup bread crumbs
4 ounces cheddar cheese, grated or cut in thin slices
Put oil in skillet. Add all ingredients except cheese. Place skillet on stove and heat mixture thoroughly. Lay cheese on top. Cover. Turn heat to low. When cheese is melted, serve. (5 servings)

Saturday Lunch
A-to-Z soup pot (A to Z means you have cleaned out the refrigerator so you can start a clean slate for the new week.)
Salad bar
Tofu dressing*
Freshly baked whole-wheat rolls (You can buy them.)
2% milk
Herb tea

Tofu Dressing

(If you haven't experimented with tofu as an addition to stir-fry meals, this recipe is a good introduction.)

1/2 pound tofu
1 avocado, peeled
1 tablespoon oil
1/4 teaspoon salt
1 tablespoon minced onion
1 tablespoon lemon juice

Mash tofu and avocado together. Add all ingredients and mix. Add more lemon juice or water if too thick.

If It Has More Than 10 Ingredients, Throw It Out

"Here's a present for us," Mel said. "A free sample that came in the mail. It's something to eat."

"If it has more than 10 ingredients throw it out," I said. At the time, I was kidding. I never throw anything out.

It looked like a product that would cost 69 cents in the grocery store, and be nothing but a little flour and spices you'd use to coat chicken with before frying it.

Let me read the label. If it has more than 10 ingredients, I refuse to use it. Anything that comes in such a little package and has more than 10 ingredients is nothing but a chemical formula made in a factory.

Aha! 18 ingredients! Do I need 18 ingredients on fried chicken?

Sugar? I don't need sugar on fried chicken. Dextrin? Dextrin is another sugar. It's a form of sugar made from corn. I don't need that on my fried chicken either. Who ever heard of putting sugar on fried chicken?

Next comes modified cornstarch. What does *modified* mean? My idea is to stick to the original material as much as possible. It's safer that way. No, I don't want modified cornstarch.

Next—hydrogenated cottonseed and soybean oils. Well, how do you like that? After all these years of doctors telling us that liquid oil is much better for us than solid fats and we're just now getting accustomed to frying chicken in oil rather than solid fat, here in this box is hydrogenated cottonseed and soybean oil. Hydrogenated oil is a solid fat. It's exactly what the doctors tell us not to use. Out with it. I don't need hydrogenated oil.

What's next? Artificial color. Do I want to dye this chicken? What color? Brown? Orange? Toast color? What's wrong with the color of ordinary fried chicken? No, I don't need any dye on this chicken.

What's next? Calcium propionate. Here's a note in parentheses: (to retard spoilage). What is there to spoil in this package? The flour? The sugar? The salt? It must be the hydrogenated oils. Well, why put them in? It says on the box you have to add two tablespoons of oil anyway. You might as well add a teaspoon more—or however much is in this package.

No, I don't think I want to put calcium propionate in my stomach unless there is a good reason. Now, if I were going to cross a desert and had to carry all my food on my back—well, then I might say, "Put something in the food to keep it from going bad." No, even then I wouldn't. I would carry dry food.

Actually this package is dry food. Or it ought to be dry food. It should be flour, salt and pepper. That's all you need to coat fried chicken with.

Here's something else. TBHQ. I don't think I know that one, other than it's another preservative. Then citric acid. There are three different preservatives in this box. You'd think the chicken was in the box. Three different kinds of preservatives. And two kinds of artificial color.

I wonder if this list of 18 ingredients is more or less what is in the boxes and barrels and cartons of fried chicken you buy in the fast-food restaurants. I suppose it is. I wonder how a stomach reacts to food with three different preservatives in it. And two kinds of artificial color.

I suppose I should use this free sample. I should experiment. I should know what is going on in the world.

But I do love my stomach. I don't want to mistreat it.

"Out out out!" I said to Mel. "Let's throw this box out." We don't fry chicken any more anyway.

Cold Turkey on Junk Food

"I went cold turkey on junk food," the student said to me as we met on the University of Montana library stairs.

"You did?" I said. "How did you feel?"

"I was a bit high-strung, nervous. You know how people talk about sugar highs. Well, I suppose I'd been on a sugar high for years. I guess I was kind of addicted. It took a while for me to get over that. I'd go by a Coke machine and look at it and want one."

"You can get along now without candy and soft drinks?" I asked.

"It's not as hard as I thought," he said.

"Do you drink coffee?"

"Some," he said. "Mostly after dinner at night—to be social. And it tastes good."

"You can get up and get going in the morning without coffee?" I asked.

"Yes," he said. "Hey, you know what I'm into? Rose hip tea. I like it."

The wonders of the world, I said to myself as I went on up the stairs. Here's John, a six-foot young man who looks like a football player, and he stops me in the library to tell me he's drinking rose hip tea.

How far this was from that famous Latin American dinner party where I served buttered Swiss chard to the Spanish-speaking guests. Like a good American mother, I said to the gentleman on my right: "Eat your greens. They're good for you."

He looked at me with a horrified expression on his face. He drew himself up sharply and said, "*Senora,* in all my life I have never eaten anything that was good for me."

Of course it was my fault for making a remark like that at a dinner party. And to a Latin American man. It's a wonder he didn't throw the Swiss chard out the window.

But didn't we have that same kind of backlash right here in the United States where we are accustomed to doing things that are "good for us"? Wasn't there a song about a junk-food junkie who ate bean sprouts by day and candy bars by night?

I don't think we really know how people feel about nutrition. You can find statistics to prove anything you want:

a) Fast-food restaurants are expanding like mad.

b) People are more interested in healthful diets than ever before.

I like to think there are millions of high-school students like those in my friend Lillian's home-economics class. "They're soaking up what I tell them," Lillian said. "They want to learn about nutrition. They want to know what foods they should eat."

It also seems the kids are willing to do for themselves. They're willing to cook.

Maybe the the wheel goes around, the pendulum swings the other way, and a generation of kids will come along who will say, "There must be more to food than fried chicken and hamburgers."

My student friend John has graduated from school by now. Maybe he's working in a place with unlimited coffee perking night and day (terrible idea) and free sticky doughnuts on trays going by his desk (don't do me that favor). But I'll celebrate that shining moment on the UM library stairs.

For one week, one month, one year—whatever—John was in charge. "Hey," he said, "I'm not some junk-food junkie. I can take it or leave it."

10 Hints for Losing Weight

1) Eat lightly and leave home.
    Don't sit and knit.
    Go
    be
    become.
    If you leave a vacuum
    food will fill it.

I went from 160 to 127, and the weight stayed off. How? I changed my whole way of life. It was as simple as that. And as complicated.

How did I get so fat? It was during my junior year in college. I was studying home economics. I took a course in quantity cookery and I ate all the cookery. I ate myself from 115 to 125 to 135. Then I graduated and went to California, but I kept on eating. I sat on the beach and ate. I wrote poetry and ate. I read books and ate.

I was fat for six years. I lost it in one year, in New York. Looking for jobs, getting fired, fighting the subway.

Besides working, I became a joiner. Hiking clubs, exercise clubs, dance clubs, little-theatre clubs. I was out every night. Well, I was only 25 and I had all this energy—160 pounds of it.

I had no time to eat—literally. But what I did eat was plain, good food. Mostly vegetables. I'm convinced that vegetables are the key. You can eat tons. You get all kinds of vitamins and minerals, enzymes, lots of roughage. And I think there are substances in vegetables that cut down your appetite.

But the main thing is you have to redo your thinking. You have to put something in your life that takes the place of eating. When you leave home what will you do? You can't go to a Cookie Exchange.

> *So*
> *Hike*
> > *dance*
> > > *sing*
> > > > *act.*
> *Take a class,*
> > *give a class.*
> *Join a political party.*
> *Be a REVOLUTIONARY!*
> *How many FAT REVOLUTIONARIES*
> *do you know?*

2) Throw out all of your women's magazines. They'll drive you schizo. Page 1 is a diet. Page 2 is a chocolate cake. It's a no-win situation.

3) Change friends if necessary. Look for non-eaters. Look for DOers.

4) Sleep less. No napping. After dinner walk out the door and lock it behind you.

5) Eat before you go out to eat, then just nibble. The first U.S. ambassador I met in South America (the one in Santiago, Chile) always did that. He said, "Doctor's orders."

6) Dilute your food. My nephew Jay once named me, "The Great Diluter."

"She'll come and pour water in the orange juice," he said. "Then she'll dilute the whole milk with skim milk. She'll add an extra can of water to the mushroom soup. She'll dilute the meat loaf with oatmeal. She'll make five cups of tea from one teabag."

"I'm diluting my life," I said, "so it'll go farther."

7) Eat oatmeal—good, cheap and filling. While I was losing weight in New York I ate a whole pot of oatmeal every night before I went to

bed—after dancing, hiking, acting and riding the subway in the cold depths of midnight.

8) Avoid diet foods like the plague. They create disharmony in the stomach. They create cravings and addictions. Eat a turnip, or whole-wheat bread, or any good, solid food.

> *Go ahead, binge—*
> *on raw sunflower seeds,*
> *apples,*
> *and a pot of oatmeal*
> *with nothing on it.*

9) Sweat. Exercise is a must. You don't want loose skin hanging like a shower curtain.

10) Leave the scales alone. Don't step on them every five minutes. You have better things to do. DO is the key. Start a Saturday Morning Walking Club. Count the butterflies in your neighborhood.

Clothes & Fashion

Thank You Hippies

for freeing me
from girdles
92-piece china sets
40-dollar crocodile bags,
shoes to match.
When I think of the time I have spent
matching hose to slip to blouse
the basic suit
the travel suit
the theater suit
the little black dress
the gloves milady wears
the pearls.
When I think of the time I have spent
when I might have been tutoring a child
writing a poem
reading a book.
The hippies broke the mold.
Let us sit on the floor and listen
to the winding of our heart.

How I Dropped Fashion.
Or Did Fashion Drop Me?

The day my name was mentioned in *Time* magazine I picked my winter wardrobe out of my neighbor's trash can.

I was walking down the alley to check on an apple tree that hung over the fence in the alley. I never pick fruit off a privately owned tree, but if it falls on the ground in an alley, I feel it then becomes an alley apple. And alley apples belong to people who walk through alleys.

What should I see in this alley but a whole armload of clothes draped across the trash can in back of a house belonging to some people very well known in town.

I wasted not one moment in picking up the whole armload of clothes, plus two pairs of shoes.

Everything fit me perfectly. Well, the lady of the house is my size exactly. And she buys very good clothes. I would never have a pair of shoes like these—soft suede, thick soles—so warm and comfortable. I looked forward to putting them on when I went home.

Of course each item in the trash can had a flaw, or a hole, or a torn seam, but I can certainly fix that. One of the shoes needed a new eyelet. Mel attached it in a second. A shirt, a lovely tan and brown plaid overblouse, the kind I'd never go downtown and buy for myself, had one sleeve out of the socket. I had to sew it back in and attach a patch to strengthen it. I can see where the original owner of this shirt could not go around with a sewed-up sleeve strengthened with a patch. That would never do. It would have to be invisibly mended by a tailor. And who in this day and age can afford a tailor? Much simpler to buy a new blouse.

Besides, a person gets tired of the same old clothes. Even I pass on clothes once in a while. Yes, I actually fill a box and take it to a church rummage sale. No doubt my contribution goes straight into the 10-cents-a-pound cleaning rags, but I don't need to know that. Better than throwing them in *my* trash can. I simply couldn't do that. I could put them on top of the trash can as my neighbor did. I wonder if she hoped someone would come by and make use of this wardrobe?

I won't mention it to her if we meet somewhere. I doubt that's done. If we do meet and I have on her shirt, I'll ignore it. She probably will too.

Although she might mention the pin attached to the shirt. There is a small, gold-plated pin attached to the blouse. Was that pin meant to be thrown out along with the blouse? I don't know.

It's still attached. If the lady and I ever meet and she looks at the pin, I'll pass it right over. I don't need it. I never wear pins.

In addition, there was a good pair of blue jeans and two knit golfing shirts. I don't golf, but the shirts will do fine for jogging or tennis or backpacking or under a sweater.

I love inheriting clothes. It's like a Christmas package. Or maybe it takes me right back to the missionary barrels we had as children.

I don't know why we called them *missionary barrels.* Actually they were cardboard boxes of old clothes that people donated to us during the Depression. There were many poor families in our township, but there were also families who were not poor. I don't know whether the boxes of clothes came from the well-off families of the township or from some organized relief agency. All I remember is that from time to time large cardboard boxes of old clothes arrived at our small farm.

I don't remember being ashamed. No doubt later on in life I had twinges, maybe during my high-school days. But if so, they didn't produce a major trauma.

The picture grooved deepest in my mind shows me digging joyously through the boxes and putting on fantastic outfits. I wish I had kept some of them. I distinctly remember some fringed red silk. It probably was a '20s flapper dress. I wish it were hanging in my closet right now. I'd wear it to a Halloween masquerade party. Or maybe I'd wear it to *any* party—a tea party or the opening of an art show at the museum.

I remember a lavender wool skirt with pleats in it. It would be right in fashion now. I should have kept it. I think I did take it along to college.

Of course I felt out of step at college. I went to Cornell University straight from the little, rock-hill farm in the Hudson Valley, at 16. I thought I would change into a sorority girl overnight, with hair shining in the sun.

No doubt I thought clothes were all that stood between me and Prince Charming. Clothes were important in those days—the '40s—but not that important. In my senior year I bought my wardrobe in New York City but by then I'd given up on being a sorority girl and settled for being a bookworm. I was a bookworm reading Spinoza.

After graduating from college I went to California to seek my fortune. I never found any fortune, not even a good job. Certainly not a Prince Charming. I dreamed on the shore at Carmel, waited table in Palm Springs, was a copygirl on the old *Los Angeles Examiner.*

I alternated spurts of Bullock's tailored suits with blue jeans. Sometimes I walked barefoot through Westlake Park. Sometimes I wore three-inch heels on Wilshire Boulevard.

It was during this period that I came home one evening from a long walk on the beach and wrote a poem to myself:

> *You are a mudpond—*
> *stagnant.*

With that I took the Greyhound bus across the continent back to where I started from.

I didn't have a career in New York either, but I managed to find a job and a husband. The husband took me to South America, where we lived the expatriate country-club life.

We went home every three years. I shopped on Fifth Avenue—little black dresses, the theater suit, four evening gowns. On sale. I did manage to retain that much sanity.

How did I get from the country club in Santiago, Chile, to a trash can in an alley in Missoula, Montana? I think I peeled off layers like an onion and now I am back to where I was a thousand years ago on a rock-hill farm in the Hudson valley.

We left our home in South America rather hastily, so we had to set up a new home in Montana and outfit ourselves with a whole new wardrobe of clothes quite different from what we wore in Chile.

We arrived back in the United States in 1971. The U.S. was in the throes of affluence. Furniture, clothes, gadgets were walking around the streets looking for new owners. For free. People didn't even want money. They just wanted to get rid of the stuff.

We furnished our whole house with leftovers from my husband's family. We didn't buy a piece of furniture.

At first I looked in stores for a Montana-type wardrobe, but one Saturday morning a friend said, "Want to go rummaging?" and that was the end of store-buying. After living in South America for 18 years where nothing was thrown out—we reused pickle jars until they were worn out—to go to 15 rummage sales in one day and see brand-new items pressed on you for 50 cents made my head spin.

It also made my hands reach out and pluck. I plucked until I filled my closets. Now I have clothes for all seasons. I have shoes for all occasions.

Of course these shoes aren't always what the "well-dressed woman" would have on her feet. One day I found myself at a City Spirit meeting with bowling shoes on. My neighbor at the conference table remarked, teasingly—he's a friend of mine—"Nice bowling shoes you're wearing."

"Thank you," I said.

Why was I wearing bowling shoes to the City Spirit meeting when it was a dressed-up meeting in a downtown motel? During intermission I explained the discrepancy to my conference neighbor. The meeting was a mile and a half from my home, but I wanted to walk. I couldn't wear heels, and I certainly didn't want to wear my hiking boots, jogging shoes or tennis sneakers. A person doesn't want to look counterculture at a Chamber of Commerce-type meeting.

I was not in corduroy or blue jeans. I was wearing polyester pants and a polyester shirt. My sister bought the shirt for me. She insisted on buying it—for $18. I told her not to do it. "I can buy all the polyester shirts I want for 50 cents in a church sale," I said. I wanted her to send that $18 to Common Cause, the Environmental Information Center or one of those Alliances fighting nuclear power.

"That's fine," my sister said, but she bought the shirt anyway. So I have this navy-blue polyester shirt to wear on certain occasions along with off-white polyester pants—off-white not from choice but from years of service. Polyester never wears out, but the white does get off-white. Some people mind. I don't.

Anyway, I have this blue-and-white outfit and I think the bowling shoes go well with it. They're tan, soft leather, very comfortable.

And I paid only 25 cents for them at the Senior Citizens rummage sale.

I must admit I thought my feet might dissolve or rot off when I bought my first pair of rummage sale shoes. But nothing happened. So now I have 20 pairs of rummage sale shoes, average cost 25 cents, and two pairs of alley shoes, which cost nothing.

Alleys are monuments to the throw-away society. You can find anything you want. One day I said to my husband, "I'd like a lamp for my desk." I went out walking and had my choice of two. It is amazing how many lamps are standing around in alleys, just leaning against garbage pails.

All our lawn furniture was leaning against garbage pails once. In an affluent society, when the plastic webbing on a lawn chair gives way, out goes the lawn chair.

I am happy to report there are fewer lawn chairs leaning against garbage pails than there used to be. This means that people are starting to reweave the plastic bottoms instead of buying new chairs. This is a good sign. Throwing out perfectly good aluminum frames just because the webbing is gone is foolish.

I know we don't go around today saying "A penny saved is a penny earned," and I know that if all people found their chairs and lamps in the alley and bought their shoes for 25 cents and their shirts for 50 cents something terrible would happen (or would have happened) to the state of the economy in this country. A businessman said that to me. I remember it very well. It made a great impression on me. "Kim Williams," he said, "you are economically inactive." He said it as though I might as well be dead. I was of no use whatsoever in this whole wide world. I was not buying. I was not making the wheels of progress go around.

That was 15 years ago. I'm still economically inactive. But I wonder—If I send the $18 that I'm not spending on the shirt and the $29.95 that I'm not spending on the shoes to the League of Women Voters or Save the Children—doesn't it end up in the gears of the economy? I'll have to think about that.

I suppose I should also think about fashion. What would happen to fashion if people wore bowling shoes to go shopping? Or to teach school? The world might fly apart.

KIM WILLIAMS'

The Truth Is You Can Get Pregnant In a Granny Gown

When the stores say, "Buy this nightgown!"
and you look at it and it's a wisp
of cold clammy nylon
and you're trying to lower your utility bill,
do you buy that nightgown or do you say
"Look, brother, are you trying
to give me pneumonia?
Are you trying to kill me off?"

You can pay $50
for hiking boots.
You can pay $150.
You can pay $5 at a rummage sale.
The score is still three to one:
buy three, get one that fits.
Dusty Farnham climbed St. Mary's peak barefoot.
The Indians walked on their feet
and their arches didn't collapse.
Are our genes different?
Have they been hybridized?

Money

"You don't buy, you don't sell.
You don't wheel, you don't deal.
No credit cards, no driver's license. DO YOU EXIST?"

"Lucy," I said, "My real life is to live in a convent—to read, write and think."
"That's not a convent," Lucy said. "You want to be the queen bee."

Money is a tool. I have that pasted on my mirror.
Don't die rich. I have that pasted on my mirror.
But how rich?
I WANT TO THROW DOLLAR BILLS IN THE AIR.

MONEY—getting it, keeping it, spending it—don't let it rule your life.

Don't die poor. I have that pasted on my mirror.

Thornton Wilder wore unmatched clothes and gave money away.

Mother Nature, if I learn the herbs will someone bring me a bowl of food and a woven shirt?

The Welfare Christmas Party

Trixie, I think you know how to deal with money. What did you say one day? Yes, I remember. You said, "There's one thing I want to be very sure about. I don't want the children to grow up and have every single thing in their life hinge on BECAUSE WE DON'T HAVE MONEY."

Oh wise and wonderful Trixie. Your Christmas party made a great impression on me. Oh, I know it wasn't your party. It was your children's. *Come to a Christmas play,* the invitation said. *With Music and Dance. And Refreshments.* (They were healthful refreshments too. Thank you, children of the wise and wonderful Trixie.)

The play was wise and wonderful too. It was Christmas Eve, and the children were anxious for Christmas morning and presents. But there were no presents.

The characters in the play were the mother, the maid and three children. Why a maid in this poverty family? What a touch! A stroke of genius! Your children will go far, Trixie. The mother, the maid and the three children wake up on Christmas morning but no miracle happened. There are no presents. What to do? Go to the piano, sing to the day and its dawning. Sing because you have a voice and you can sing. So starkly simple and beautiful. I had tears in my eyes, Trixie.

"I didn't write the play," you said. "I didn't teach them that. Of course I buy them presents. But we also sing and dance."

The program said—

SETTING: A cold Christmas Eve in a small house, followed by Christmas morning

MORAL OF THE STORY: Don't count on Santa to bring happiness

The mother in the play was labeled *SERENE: A Maiden.* A jade plant was the Christmas tree. A missionary barrel furnished the dress-up clothes. But the piano was real. The singing was real.

The NARRATOR narrated: "And they all learned to give love instead of presents and were very happy."

How can anyone top that? Oh wise and wonderful Trixie.

Coupons Are
a Communist Plot

Mel was opening the mail. "What's this?" he asked.

"It's a refund check," I said.

A slip of paper in the envelope said, *THANKS FOR BUYING OUR PRODUCT. HERE'S YOUR CHECK FOR THE VO-5 HAIRDRESSING REFUND OFFER.*

"How much is it for?" Mel asked.

"50 cents," I said.

"Minus 22 cents for the stamp," Mel said.

I don't know why I keep doing this. For 28 cents—no, less actually because there's the cost of the envelope too. For about 26 cents I waste time cutting a refund coupon off a box. Sometimes I even run to the store for a certificate or official form.

I don't know why I do it and I don't know why the companies do it. Look at this VO-5 business. A check was made out—for 50 cents— by the Citizens State Bank of Waterville, MN. For 50 cents someone had to make up that check, put it in an envelope, take it to the post office and mail it. The VO-5 company had to pay postage. The post office had to sort the envelope, put it on a plane or train, bring it to Missoula, sort it again, put it in a mailperson's sack and that person had to bring it to our door.

Isn't this all a lot of nonsense? I mean real non-sense. You know very well the VO-5 company could just lower the price of the product by 26 cents. Or put a coupon right in the package. Why all this cutting and pasting and mailing to and fro?

Why doesn't the post office holler? "Hey, VO, we got more to do than participate in nonsense."

And the bank. Why doesn't the bank holler?

I think there's more here than meets the eye. It's a plot to keep all of us housewives, househusbands, bank people, post office people so busy we don't have time to think about big things. I mean—here I am cutting and pasting and mailing coupons for 26 cents when I should be asking the President, "WHAT ARE YOU DOING, MAN?"

Banking's Stuffed Owls

I started losing faith in the white-hot wisdom of banks when my house began filling up with stuffed owls.

I remember saying to my bank, "Another present?"

"Take it. It's free," the teller said.

I already had a stadium blanket, a paring knife, an electric clock, a frying pan, a set of bowls, a cutlery set, an umbrella and two radios with very poor tone.

I approached an official-looking person sitting at a desk 10 feet square. You can't get too close. Beside the enormous desk was a big green philodendron—very shiny, as though somebody had cleaned the leaves with milk that very day.

I parted the philodendron and said timidly, "Maybe you could just give us a little more interest."

The man was very polite. He smiled beneficently. But of course the interest stayed the same.

The next week there was a barbecue—an entire side of beef on a spit to commemorate the opening of a new branch in the shopping center. Full-page ads in the newspaper bannered: *COME AND LUNCH ON US!*

"Let's do it," I said to Mel.

"Thanks," he said, "but I'll have my sandwich and watch the ballgame."

So I went with Trixie and her three children. There was a long line, but we ate meat and corn and rolls and cheese, then cake, coffee and soda pop—the works.

I ran into Louie of Mecklesby Advertising Agency. I knew Louie from my stint of civic duty on the Local Government Study Commission. He had helped us publicize our home-rule charter, which failed. But it wasn't Louie's fault.

"Louie," I now said, "are you working for this bank?"

"In a way," he said.

"Well, why not just give us a little more interest on our money?"

Louie wasn't fazed at all. PR man to the core, he retorted, "If you're complaining, why are you standing in line eating free barbecue?"

Why was I? Two hours later I thought of the right answer. "TO COLLECT MY MONEY!" That's what I should have said.

The Lost-Cause Calendar

I ran into my Montana Congressman Pat Williams at a political meeting.

"Hi, Pat," I said. "Guess what is on the wall of my kitchen. Your calendar—the one with the pictures of the Capitol on it. It's very nice, but you remember I asked you not to send me any more calendars. I was thinking of the cost to us taxpayers. There's the cost of printing plus the postage. Oh, I guess you don't pay postage. But the postal workers don't work for free. Someone is paying them to lug around these big, heavy calendars."

Pat Williams: "I'll take you off the list, Kim, but people like those calendars."

Me: "Oh, here's Gertrude and Tom. Gertrude, do you want these Congressional calendars even though they are at taxpayers' expense and you can get all the calendars you want free from banks, insurance companies and service stations?"

Gertrude: "Pat, can we have two calendars this year? My son wants one for his office."

Lois's Worm Boots
Are True Barter

Lois, I think barter works better for you than for me. I remember your worm boots. That's what you called them.

You kicked up your heels at the trailhead meeting spot of our "Women on Wednesday" hiking group. "See my worm boots?" you said.

Of course we said, "What do you mean—worm boots?"

"Well, I wanted these Army-surplus hiking boots that I saw at the Army/Navy store," you said, "but I didn't have the $23."

This is what barter is all about. If you want something and you don't have the cash flow—as they say—what you do is trade something you have and the other person doesn't have.

What Lois had were worms. Her backyard was full of earthworms—night crawlers—the kind people buy to go fishing with at 60 cents a dozen.

As Lois put it, she didn't dream that the owner of the store would accept worms. She thought of strawberry jam or chocolate-chip cookies, but his wife was in charge of that department. So Lois shrugged and said, "Well, the only other thing I have is a garden full of earthworms."

"Now you're talking," the store owner said. He didn't want the worms for fishing. Or to sell. No. He wanted them for a turtle. His son had won a turtle, a large turtle, in a school contest, and he was feeding the turtle three earthworms in the morning and three at night—night crawlers six inches long.

"I'll throw in a tub," Lois said. "I have a tub I got in a rummage sale."

"It's a deal," the store man said.

Lois delivered the worms in two batches. The first batch was (so she said) 169-1/2 worms. The half was just for fun. Lois says she pulled and pulled—just like a robin—and the worm stretched to one foot long but she still got only half of it.

One month later Lois delivered the second batch of 169-1/2 worms. "It was easy," she said. "I've got a gold mine in my backyard."

She'll probably trade worms for something else some day. Maybe a butter churn. Or a front door.

Low-Cost (?) Wart Removal

It costs more to have a wart removed by tying a thread around it than it does using a chemical. I was really surprised. But the nurse at the University Health Service proved it to me.

I dropped in at the clinic and showed the nurse a wart on my neck. It was the skinny kind, a sort of tag hanging on by practically nothing. "Can you tie a thread around it?" I asked. "I've done it myself before but this one is on my neck where I can't reach it, and my husband is farsighted. The procedure is really quite easy," I said to the nurse.

"Wouldn't you rather I used liquid air?" the nurse asked.

"What's liquid air?" I asked. "Is it a chemical?"

"It burns the wart right off."

"I'd rather you just tied a thread around it," I said.

"I don't have any thread," she answered.

"Oh," I said.

"Well, I could go to the doctor and get some surgical thread but he'll give me a hard time. Surgical thread costs money."

"Oh," I said. "Never mind then."

"Well, wait here."

So I waited, and she came back to tie a surgical thread around the wart. A week later the wart, thread and all, was gone. Fait accompli. Case closed.

But it isn't just the University Health Service that can't deal with thread around a wart. Dr. Donohue, who writes a syndicated health column, has no thread either. I quote him in answer to a reader who asked how she could get rid of the same kind of wart I had. They're called *skin tags*.

Dr. Donohue answered: *Skin tags can be removed by cutting them off, either by electric current or by freezing them.*

You can also, as per Tom Sawyer and Huck Finn, go to the cemetery at midnight and swing a dead cat around your head. But why not just tie a simple white thread around the warts?

Some of the Best Things in Life Are Free

I looked at my wallet one day. It was dusty. I hadn't used it for so long that even though it was inside my dresser drawer it had collected a thin film of dust.

I literally hadn't spent a cent in months. But I was not home in bed bemoaning high prices. I was out of the house from morning to night having a wonderful time.

Is it possible to enjoy life without spending money on that enjoyment? I say it is.

Naturally my husband and I spend money: on taxes, our car, our home, utilities, health care, food staples, even wine for dinner.

"Mel, how much do we spend a year?" I asked my husband when I was writing this.

"What we need," he answered.

"What's the figure?"

"I never figure it."

It's probably poverty level. Maybe below.

Actually it's the money we *don't* spend above the basic food-and-shelter level that I'm talking about here. And the fact that we're living what I think is a rich life. We don't feel deprived. We're part of the community—with friends, social ties, involvement.

The future might well be a time when more people have to deal with a smaller income. I say that you don't have to settle for a small life just because your income is small.

"The best things in life are free," my friend Margaret England wrote me from San Francisco. She doesn't really believe that and neither do I, but her idea was that some things in life are free and you might as well find those things.

After our house in Missoula was stuffed as full as anyone else's with rummage-sale or hand-me-down furniture and clothes—even pictures for the wall—I turned my attention to wants and desires other than physical. I looked for entertainment, conversation, knowledge.

All this is out there and it's free.

In one week I went to a symphony concert, a poetry reading, a lecture on world affairs, a lecture on the Supreme Court, a museum reception, and a coffee-and-cookie open house at a new furniture store.

My husband was out of town then, so I practically shut up the house and lived away from home. Think how valuable that could be if times get really tough. A person on a fixed income could shut the thermostat down to 49° and bask in the warmth of public buildings.

I shut off the hot-water heater too. Why have a huge tank of hot water if no one is using it? I'm a perennial student, so I have an I.D. card that is "open-sesame" to gyms, showers, libraries, typewriters, reading rooms—the whole university world.

Even if you aren't a student, the university world is wide open and essentially free. Anyone can use the library. Anyone can attend recitals, art shows, plays, lectures. There are so many free lectures going on around any university that you can get an entire education without even registering.

If your city or town doesn't have a university, it will still have lectures, art shows, educational films and slide shows.

And of course there is the public library—the great, marvelous, not-able-to-be-overestimated institution of the American public library.

We don't appreciate this institution enough. Many people never use the public library!

I always have. All my life the first thing I did in any town was to find out where the public library was.

Maybe it started with the Eureka-like discovery at age seven that there were books in the world. My Hungarian immigrant family did not buy or own books. It was in a one-room country school with its 12 or 15 library books that I discovered the world-shaking phenomenon of free reading. I mean fiction reading, not grammar books, not primers, not arithmetic, geography and history. These library books were fiction books and they were free for us to read.

Then my eldest sister, Froni, brought home a bonanza when she worked in a city 20 miles from our farm. She worked in the public library there and one year they cleaned out the old books. Froni volunteered to take them, or maybe she asked for them. Anyway, a hundred books arrived at our farm.

Three tremendous things resulted from this happening:

1) I became educated. I literally believe that. I honestly think my education started with those hundred books. From then on I always seemed to know as much as—or more than—I was supposed to know for my age and background.

2) I ruined my eyes. I read from morning to night.

3) I became a thing apart from the rest of the family. No one could find me. I was under the bed, behind the dresser, off in a cow pasture—with a book. My father screamed; my mother yelled. Now that I look back I can't understand why they didn't throw out all the books. Why didn't my father simply build a huge bonfire and get rid of all those distractions from the business of doing chores in a family with seven children during the Depression years?

I am still a public-library person. I love libraries. I thank our government for libraries. I appreciate living in the United States of America because of libraries. And universities, and community colleges, and free public schools, and scholarships.

I have made use of all these amenities of life. I shall continue until the day I die. I buy no books. None. I buy no magazines. I have no subscriptions. I know that is terrible to say. Who will support the bookstores and the publishers of wonderful books and magazines— some on a shoestring?

I am sorry about this, but I am telling it as it is. I don't buy books. I don't subscribe to magazines. I don't pay for cable TV.

If everyone did as I do, would the world come to a screaming halt? I don't know. Perhaps we would recover the oral tradition. I could tell stories to children. Other people could.

I could even help print books if I had to. I don't know what I could or would do under different circumstances. I'm merely saying how I do things in the time and era I'm living in now.

I have more time than money. Therefore I'm adopting a lifestyle that takes into account a person getting ready to retire in an era that was very affluent and is about to become less so. But the paraphernalia of this era is still very much around waiting to be used, enjoyed and appreciated.

I hope that without shame or false pride many, many people will do as I do—take what's offered by this still-affluent society. Use it, appreciate it, say thank you. You don't always have to make return in the form of money.

Meeting People & Making Friends

*One thing leads to another.
Nothing happens if you're glued
to your four walls and the TV.*

Like a Cabbage
I Was "For Sale"

It was the hat that did it. I put it on my head and walked into this church where I knew nobody. Nobody. I didn't even know anything about the church. Actually it was a Fellowship, the Unitarian Fellowship of Missoula.

I wasn't a Unitarian. I didn't even know what a Unitarian was. I'd spoken to one once in Santiago, Chile. He was with U.S. AID. He invited me to a sort of open house on a Sunday afternoon at his home. I thought the whole bunch was off the wall—far out—a bunch of bleeding hearts, flying around in some never-never land.

So why was I going to a Sunday morning meeting with my black-felt derby on my head?

For one plain and simple reason. Mel and I were new in town. We had come like Little Orphan Annie to stay in this town of Missoula, Montana, after 18 years in South America—me a New Yorker, Mel a Montanan but not from Missoula. And besides, he'd been gone for 30 years.

When you don't know anybody, you have to start somewhere. So I looked up churches in the newspaper. (Always subscribe to the local newspaper the first day on arriving in town.) I looked under churches and—how can I say this?—I looked for those within walking distance. Well no, not really, although it might have had a little bit to do with my choice.

I walked into the church and sat down. At the end of the service I walked up to the group gathered around the coffee urn and said hello.

In a way I announced myself, as much as to say, "I'm here. I'm new in town."

I'm not going to say that a Sunday meetingplace is open-sesame to health, wealth and happiness—14 friendships, 15 invitations to teas, coffees, lunch and dinners.

But it is a group of people. I found that in this Unitarian Fellowship I could do as much or as little as I wanted. And I could do it by myself. Mel did not accompany me. "What! You didn't urge him?" you'll say. No, I didn't urge him. It wouldn't have done a bit of good. You can tell Mel to his face, "You're a mule." You can tell him to his face, "Even an old dog learns some new tricks." It won't change anything.

I went by myself, and I made friends. I could have become a pillar of the community if I'd so desired.

Actually the church wasn't the first thing I tried. The very first was also from the newspaper, from a column of *Goings-On-Around Town*. There's always that kind of a column. Sure enough, the second day we were in Missoula, I was at a dessert-and-coffee for newcomers at the Holiday Inn.

I haven't done such a thing since—pay money to stuff myself with ice cream, cake and coffee. But I had a purpose in mind, and I did it. I paid $1.75 to drink too much strong coffee and eat too sweet a dessert. But I accomplished what I set out to do: I met someone. At this very first meeting, the first and last newcomers dessert I attended, I met Myra, who was a "young married." I was a "middle-aged married," but we met anyway and we've been friends ever since.

Myra and I laugh about our meeting. She was operating under the same rules. That was her first and last attendance. She too is averse to paying money for dessert and coffee. But she did it for the same reason I did.

Another reason we laugh is that we met ostensibly to play tennis. When I stood up and announced that I was looking for a tennis game, Myra raised her hand, then came over during the "mix-and-chat" time. It turned out she didn't really care about tennis, but she thought we might visit anyway. Then we found out her husband and my husband both liked to hike and they played bridge. So it turned out fine, even though we are in different generations. We all joined the Rocky Mountaineers Hiking Club and that of course led to more friendships.

The third group I joined right there that first week in town was a poetry club. It happened while I was attending a session of the local bridge club. I was introduced as a newcomer, and I stood up and announced my interests.

You have to do this. Don't slide into the drapes, hem and haw around, blush, giggle or faint. Just announce your interests in a calm voice.

And smile. After all, you are laying a cabbage on the marketstand. You're the cabbage. Don't follow the example of the Frenchman in the old joke who went from his province to Paris looking like a rumpled old shoe. When a friend remonstrated with him, saying that he dressed like a rag at home and now he was doing the same in the big city, he said, "Everyone knows me at home so why dress up? And in Paris nobody knows me so what difference does it make?" That's not for you. The Frenchman wasn't selling or buying.

When you're new in town, you're selling. You want to be bought. So put a ribbon in your hair. I put lipstick on, and nylons. I was selling myself as a newcomer.

A lady at the bridge club invited me to a meeting of the poetry club. I liked the group. We wrote and discussed poetry.

Later on I joined the university—took classes, planned a master's degree. That turned into all kinds of things. I am now teaching in summer school. My commentaries on National Public Radio started at the university. I was doing a local program for the university station. The station director sent a tape to *All Things Considered*.

In New York when I was single, I followed the same pattern—after I saw the light and came up out of the public library's book stacks. I joined everything in sight—even a dude ranch. I met a woman named Marian who frequented a dude ranch—in Peekskill of all places. I couldn't believe it, but I went with Marian and liked it. We spent all our weekends and all our money for a solid year.

Then I met Mel. Now, don't follow me in this instance. I met Mel in a nightclub. Nobody meets anyone in a nightclub—to marry. I know my father said, "Even a blind chicken finds a grain of corn once in a while." BUT DON'T YOU DO IT. DON'T EXPECT TO FIND A LASTING PARTNER IN A BAR OR NIGHTCLUB.

Oh, I suppose you can break all the rules once in a while. But you have to be willing to be shattered—busted into little pieces. And you have to say to yourself, "I can pick up my own pieces."

10 Ways to Start Meeting and Greeting

1) Leave home. Go looking. The only people who come looking for you buried in your house are burglars and intruders.

2) Look at yourself in the mirror and ask yourself honestly: "What do I have to offer?" I had a friend in South America who said she invited more people to her house than invited her back. Sometimes you have to do that.

On the other hand, my friend Vera was invited EVERYWHERE, and it didn't matter if she ever threw any bash bigger than a backyard lemonade and bean dip. But Vera was the type who could walk down Florida Street in Buenos Aires with a bundle of gladiolas in her arms and collect a string of followers like the Pied Piper of Hamlin. Vera could play the guitar. She could dance the flamenco. She could laugh. She could even cook.

And she was a FRIEND when you needed a FRIEND. When I had a miscarriage, she took me to the hospital (Mel was out of town) and then spent the night with me right there in my room. People did that in South America. It was allowed.

3) Sit down and write a résumé—not for a job but for a friendship. If you have nothing but blank spaces on the sheet you can start now and work on it. Learn something for the next time you write your Résumé for a Friendship.

4) Start with acquaintances—don't ask for friends. They might turn into friends, but if they don't, acquaintances might be all you need.

5) Make a list of all the clubs, groups, organizations in your community—then ask yourself, "What's in it for me?" It's OK to ask that. It sounds crass, but in the long run it works for you and for the organization.

Put a star near the DOING types of organizations. Making small talk while sitting with your hands folded is a bore. You will do better hiking or stuffing envelopes for a political campaign or delivering meals-on-wheels with a partner.

The same is true of taking a course. Pick one that's a workshop, so you don't sit and listen to a professor lecture. You meet people by DOING THINGS TOGETHER. (Be leary of applying this rule to bar-hopping—ahem!)

6) Learn the Basic Social Skills. Make a list.

> *What can I do?*
> *a) Cook*
> *b) Ski*
> *c) Play tennis*
> *d) Play bridge*
> *e) Help a child learn to read*
> *f) Tutor in Spanish*
> *g) Tutor in math*
> *h) Insulate a house*
> *i) Paint a house*
> *j) Garden*

A very basic interaction between two people is to teach someone something. You can teach for a little money in a not-for-credit evening course. Or, you can volunteer.

7) Put up with nonsense. To have friends you have to do that. Nobody is perfect. It is true that group activities can slow you down. Skiing, for instance, in a group is not as speedy and free and as much a peak-experience as being alone on the mountain. But your object here is not a peak experience of epiphany. It is down-to-earth friendship. Committee meetings can drive you crazy, but loneliness can too. You simply have to put up with BOTHER.

8) Don't fight with all your relatives. Relatives can be friends.

And they'll hold your hand when you have been deserted by the whole world—and maybe even deserved it.

9) Don't fight with your neighbors. The students who live across our alley keep breaking down our back fence. It's not their fault. Their landlord should have left more room for cars. I said to Mel, "Shall we FIGHT with them?"

"Better I go to the city dump and get some new posts," Mel said. Some new *old* posts.

It turned out there was a sour-cherry tree in the students' garden, and I've had all the cherries ever since. Once you start a fight it can be a real Hatfield-McCoy feud with your grandchildren still fighting when your bones are phosphorus ash. And someone will probably cut down the cherry tree.

10) Live someplace where things are going on. You don't have to go as far as my friend Millie Dunn, who described her apartment complex like this: "It's a regular Peyton Place," and said the words with pride. But you certainly don't want to hibernate in a cellar either.

Families
&
Living Together

Blessed be he
who has a family that works—
works in the sense that
it holds in the center.
If you don't have that kind,
you have to make your own—
out of a hat, a banana skin,
whatever, whoever, is around you.

At 96, What Is Mom's Secret?

Mom, you raised seven children
on a hard-rock farm;
boiled clothes in a copper tub—
rinsed them in ice-cold water;
chased cows out of the garden;
fed chickens and pigs and sheep;
hitched up a horse to sell eggs
in town. Here you are at 96,
eating three meals a day,
no more arthritis than anyone else.
Mom, what's your secret?

I keep asking this question because how many of us will be here at 96, even with our vitamin pills, orange juice by the gallon, and 33 How-To-Take-Care-Of-Your-Health books on our shelves.

When Mom became 90 I said to my sister Froni, "It's genes." I asked Froni, "Did you meet any 100-year-olds in Mom's family when you went to Hungary?"

"Not one person Mom's age," Froni said.

Of course they might have succumbed to "trauma," as the phrase goes—one major trauma being war.

When Mom was 91 I said to Froni, "It's Mom's routine. Look how she still irons on Tuesdays."

Mom couldn't see too well even then so she ironed atrociously, but she ironed. She even ironed dish towels. All Mom's life it was . .

wash on Monday,
iron on Tuesday,
clean on Wednesday,
bake on Thursday,
mend and patch on Friday.

and woe unto anyone who tried to alter the routine.

"There must be more to it than that," Froni said.

When Mom was 92, I said to Froni, "It's the way Mom dresses. She wears a hat. She wears cotton stockings. She wears a blouse over her dress."

"You will do the same," Froni said.

We laughed because of course I was already doing the same.

When Mom was 93, I said, "Froni, it's the twinkle in Mom's eye. She enjoys things. She laughs. She chuckles out loud when she reads the paper." (Because it was in English, she could read only half of it.)

"That can't be more than a small part of it," Froni said.

When Mom was 94, I said, "It's Mom's diet. She doesn't eat frosting." I wrote a poem about that.

> *Mom made a cake with two cups of flour,*
> *only half a cup of sugar, one egg,*
> *no frosting. She offered a piece*
> *to the neighbor. "We are accustomed,"*
> *the neighbor said, "to cakes*
> *that are richer." This neighbor*
> *is long gone. My mother*
> *is here at 96.*

Actually our family grew up with no frosting on anything. "Remember how we used to holler about the coffee?" I said to Froni. "It was all water and no coffee."

"One spoonful made a whole pot," Froni said.

"The pie crust was tough as shoe leather because it had so little fat in it," I said.

"We never won a prize at the fair for a pie," Froni said.

"We made 100 molasses cookies with 1/2 cup of fat and 1 cup of molasses," I remembered.

"It was during the Depression. Pop had no work," Froni added.

"We made two gallons of soup out of one beef bone," I said.

"It was thin soup," Froni said. "And Pop made us eat it for lunch and dinner."

"No butter on the bread," I said.

"But it was good, homemade bread," Froni said. "Mom baked every . . ."

"Thursday," I said. "Like a clock."

We laughed.

"Did we ever fry anything?" I asked. "I don't remember ever eating French fries or fried chicken."

"Never," Froni said. "One pot of fat lasted us all year."

Mom, you were ahead of your time. You raised us lean.

Mom became 96 on January 26, 1986. I wrote to Froni, "Oh my gosh, it's as clear as the nose on my face. Mom's secret is YOU. It's FAMILY. Mom has never lived away from FAMILY."

Actually it's an extended family. Through the years it has included many and varied people, but the center has always been Mom and my sister Froni, who is the eldest daughter. Froni moved out as daughters do when they go to school, get jobs and get married, but she moved back when she became divorced and had a child to support.

Here is where you might say Mom made a great decision in life. In the Biblical sense you could say she cast her bread upon the waters and it came back. Mom took in her divorced daughter for a while and that started a whole chain reaction.

When my father died, Mom moved in with Froni, who was already in an extended household. Froni's new husband, Ken, lived with a widowed sister, Irene.

Good heavens! you'll say. This is impossible. Three women in one household! There will be tearing of hair.

Maybe there was. Whoever said we should live in Perfect Peace and Harmony? That is to be found only in heaven.

But I visited that household many times, and it worked. Maybe the shape of the house had something to do with it. The house was narrow, but it had three levels. People could get away from each other.

I slept in the attic, which was my sister's hideaway. "Is this the secret of an extended family?" I asked Froni. "Each one has a hideaway?"

"You have to be polite," Froni said.

I learned about that when I visited Japan. The houses were small. The rooms were small. You took up the bed every morning and put it in a closet. You couldn't be noisy or big or jump up and down and say everything on your mind. You can only do that if you live in the wide-open spaces. In Montana, Mel and I can walk out of town into the mountains in five minutes and run and jump or holler into the skies until the clouds shake, but nobody is disturbed.

You can't do that in Japan or Singapore or Hong Kong. And you can't do it in an extended family when you live with a mother on one side and an elderly sister on the other. You have to be polite. You have to have manners.

I could see that. But I could also see that each person had a hideaway, a secret little nook to be alone in.

My sister had this sweet little attic with sky-blue-painted walls, a round braided rug on the floor and an electric typewriter humming companionably near a window looking over the Berkshire Mountains.

It didn't matter if Froni wrote letters to her son or worked on the Great American Novel. "Froni is up in the attic writing," the rest of the family said.

Maybe Froni wrote out lists of words she would say if she weren't polite. Maybe she wasn't writing at all. Maybe she was napping on the bed, which was the bed for guests or relatives or people who had to get away from other people for a while.

Mom's hideaway was her room. It was nothing big or fancy, but it was her private, not-to-be-entered-without-knocking room. It was her world with pictures of all the children, the grandchildren, the great grandchildren.

Mom could sit and rock in her private rocking chair or she could nap on the bed or look at her pictures or read her Bible that came all the way from Hungary.

Ken's hideaway was a summerhouse attached to the garage. In

winter it couldn't be used, but for spring, summer and fall Ken had a screened-in porch, a living room and even a cookstove where he baked and barbecued for picnic suppers. This was Ken's bailiwick and nobody was to enter without permission.

Ken could listen to football games or concert music. He could drink beer, smoke, dream, nap, whittle, read—anything his heart desired.

Irene had her space downstairs—a whole small apartment, but she came up for a shared meal every night. This was the time of day for talking, reading mail, making plans for birthdays, weddings—all kinds of family matters.

Money went far in this extended household. Even Social Security checks are enough if you have four of them. The utilities were paid, the house was kept up, and everyone had a little extra money to spend.

Mom still sends me money. Out of her Social Security check she sends money to children, grandchildren and great grandchildren. We send it back—on Mother's Day, on birthdays, at Christmas.

Do we have a family that works? I hope so.

KIM WILLIAMS'

My South-American Family

Family isn't just the literal family. For 18 years in South America, who was my family? You were, Lucy. I paid you, of course, but how else would I have found you? So close to my heart you were. You listened to me. I listened to you. We argued. We laughed. I'd never have made it without you.

And Vera—you and Ben and your four children—you were family. I lived at your house when Mel was out of town. I followed you around like a little sister.

Margaret and John England—you were family. You still are. "Come and stay," you say. Your heart is as big as the whole outdoors, as big as your house with seven levels. That house has room for everyone: you, John, your daughter, a son-in-law, a student from Brazil, an artist from London.

Has the artist painted that mural on your ceiling? Margaret, I name you the taker-in-er of waifs and orphans.

You fitted in so well in South America, Margaret—you and John. Did you learn "Come and stay" down there? The Latins we knew seemed to do a lot of that. If a teenager couldn't get along in her nuclear family, she went and stayed with an aunt or uncle. She didn't have to run away to Minneapolis and go into white slavery.

She didn't need to be sent to a psychiatrist either. There were always two or three in residence in those big old households. Always a grandmother, an old aunt, maybe a retired nun or priest. Don't experts say that just a listener will often do the trick?

And Jewel Goakes, you were family. You saved my life. My sanity.

You came along like a guru,
took our empty heads
and made us dance.

There we were, a bunch of bubble-headed wives of the American Women's Club of Santiago, Chile, going to teas, listening to talks by the Ambassador's wife, dancing at the country club, flirting with our husband's buddies, drinking too much, smoking too much—everything too much.

Remember the time I wore a nightgown to a dinner party? It was a costume ball at the Bellinger's and I went as Psyche—my soul—or was it the water nymph on the sparkling-water bottle. Why did I do that? Was I inviting mayhem? Was I simply bored and had to do something to liven up the routine? One was expected to live on the verge. Isn't that what the beautiful people do? They live on the crest of the wave. Or the verge of disaster?

Our friend Vincent O'Riley went to the doctor. The doctor told him to slow down. "Your liver is going," he said.

Vincent said, "Of course it's going. That's what it's for. When I die, I want my liver to be shattered. It did all it could. I did all I could."

Vincent, that's not me. I had enough. Too much. Jewel, I was ready and waiting.

"This is a Workshop of the Arts," you said. "You dance or sing or paint or write or act. There will be no small talk of maids, prices, houses, husbands, sewer systems."

Oh happy day. Oh goodbye to my past. I wrote a satire for the club to perform—about small talk of maids, prices, houses, husbands, sewer systems.

KIM WILLIAMS'

How To Live Together

I gave a talk to the YWCA Board here in Missoula, and in the middle of the talk out of my mouth came this sentence: "We need 10 lessons in how to live together." I waved a bulletin from my old alma mater, Cornell University, describing a workshop on "Shared Housing."

It's coming. I took the census in my neighborhood in 1980. I jumped up and down for months afterward. "All these people living alone!" I hollered. "All that smoke coming out of the chimney for one person, all that electricity and gas going in for one person. Where else in the world does one person have four or five or six rooms all to himself with a lighting system, a heating system, a hot-water system, a food-refrigerating system—all running-purring-humming for one person?"

And then we go to a psychologist to find out why we are lonely, blue, depressed. Nobody calls on us; nobody cares; the cold, unfeeling world has dumped on us.

But of course you can't just move people together. We are—or were—an affluent society. People are accustomed to living in regal, solitary splendor. Or maybe not so regal—maybe in an old, broken-down shack with a leaky roof—but alone, ALONE. This is my castle; draw up the drawbridge; do not enter.

One gets that way when one lives alone. One puts one's cup and saucer upside down and woe on the person who puts it any other way.

The Cornell workshop was for the bureaucracy, the agencies that will organize home-sharing programs. That's necessary.

But in addition to that type of workshop, I think we need workshops for the people who are going to live together. I know it sounds odd to have to learn to live with someone.

This learning wasn't necessary in the old days because who could afford to live alone? My mother in all her life has never lived alone.

Maybe that's why she can fit into a daughter's household. She's not accustomed to her cup upside down in her saucer.

I have never lived alone, even though I didn't get married until I was 28. Before I was married I lived with my sisters Helen and Marge in Brooklyn.

Of course we argued. We fought! "MOVE OUT! GO!" we shrieked. Nobody went. We Hungarians would rather fight than live alone. Who would we exclaim to? Ask if it's raining? Tell huge, exaggerated stories to?

The high point of our lives was Sunday-morning breakfast, after Saturday-night happenings—or non-happenings. We bought a coffeecake fresh from the bakery—all white flour and sugar, terrible! We ate toast too, even whole-wheat, but the coffeecake was a Sunday luxury. It was dessert, which, with a second pot of coffee (terrible!) held us at the breakfast table for hours while we talked over our Saturday nights. He said . . . I said . . . he said . . . I said, and so on. We gossiped; we laughed; we waited for the phone to ring.

Our married neighbors said, "This is why you girls aren't married. You're too comfortable. You have to split up."

Today I say, "Glory be! If you can find anyone to live with, even halfway comfortably—man, woman or child—go to it, GO TO IT!"

10 Rules for Living Together

1) Emulate the Japanese. Bow before speaking.

2) Go to the mountains to yell. Get it out of your system.

3) Each member of the household needs a Hideaway, a Private Space.

4) All meals need not be shared.

5) Don't sit and coffee-klatsch all day. Scatter. Regroup at dinner.

6) Remember Eunice Brown. "How are you?" is not a license to DUMP on your housemates.

7) Be a *nice* person. Are you a nice person? If not, why not?

8) Make someone laugh before the sun goes down.

9) Leave the house every day for two hours. Give your housemates a rest.

10) Learn to cook. "I can't cook" is lamebrain.

Extended Households Are for Bagel-Baking

Would you walk a mile for a Camel? Of course you wouldn't. Would you walk a mile for a bagel—a homemade bagel made of freshly ground whole-wheat flour, sourdough starter and cream cheese—with the cream cheese mixed right in the dough?

I did that—on a cold, snowy night. It was after dinner and the phone rang. Would I like to come and watch the bagels being made? I'd once said to a grad student, John, that I'd never made bagels. I knew they were rolls boiled in water then baked, but I'd never watched the operation.

"Here's your chance," John said. "Come on over."

I put on my boots with the non-slippery soles and walked over to John's house.

And that's the point of this whole story. The house wasn't John's. John lived in an extended household. The household consisted of a husband, wife and child and two graduate students.

"We've never lived alone," Lys, the wife, said. "Ever since Dan and I were married we've shared our house. Well, it's the only way we can have a house."

"Do you eat together?" I asked. "Who does the cooking? Who does the shopping?"

"Everyone chips in," Lys said.

"Nobody is the slave?" I asked.

"Everyone works or goes to school," Lys said, "so there's no one home all of the time."

"But the work gets done?" I asked.

Lys, Dan, John and Alana all laughed. "Somehow it gets done," John said.

In a university town like Missoula you expect extended households. I had a student living in our basement when Mel worked one summer in Alaska. A neighbor has a whole separate apartment in his basement. It has a private entrance. Other people rent out rooms just for sleeping and studying—no cooking.

One reason I take such a big interest in housing and living situations is that I was so amazed when I came back from living in South America. Down there I didn't know a single house that was occupied by only one person. So I was truly amazed to have people here say to me, "That's my house. I live there alone." And it would be a three-bedroom, two-story house!

Right away I would begin thinking how to remedy the situation. Do you want to take in a student? Have you got a sister? Have you got a friend?

I think in the future more and more people will be doing like Lys and Dan—rent out a room here, a room there. It helps pay the taxes. It helps pay the fuel bill.

I felt very virtuous when I had a student in the basement. When the furnace went on I said, "Aha! That heat is heating two people instead of only one. And the hot-water heater with its tank full of hot water, far too much for one person—now it's working for two."

I think I'd get spoiled if I had a whole house to myself. I'd get so set in my ways that when Mel came back he'd find all the cups labeled and the dish towels with tags saying use this one for glasses and the other one for silverware. The newspaper would be folded until noon. TV can't go on until 6 p.m.

Oh, I argued once in a while with my student. He would forget his key and I'd have to get up at 4 a.m. and let him in. But I went back to sleep. It didn't kill me to get up.

And he told me marvelous stories. Some of them were even true.

The Huckleberry Family

It wasn't Huckleberry Finn—it was the Huckleberry family.
"We've come here every summer for five years," they told me.
Mel and I were spending the weekend near Kleinschmidt Flat in the Lolo National Forest. I was walking with my tin pail.
"Any huckleberries left?" I asked as I walked by the family's camp. Four little girls flew out. "We'll show you," they said.
They not only showed me; they picked half of my berries. And they'd already picked all morning with their family.
Actually, they were *families.* This camp consisted of six adults and 11 children. Imagine 17 people spending half a week together in a wilderness camp to pick huckleberries.
. There was no lake, no river. A creek was 200 yards away through brush and tangled undergrowth. And it was too cold for wading and too small for swimming. There were plenty of mosquitoes and no place to get away from them except inside the tents. With 17 people, how much room would there be inside the tents for lounging?
"This is something I should study," I said to myself. "What is the secret of this family—this extended family?"
"She's my best friend," eight-year-old Susie said to me about eight-year-old Tamie. "We go everywhere together. We're going to have farms side by side when we grow up and get married. At first we thought we might live together with our husbands and children, but maybe her children would start calling me Mommie and mine would call her Mommie so we decided to live next door instead of together."
Is the secret good friends? Maybe mosquitoes and no swimming and picking huckleberries three days in a row aren't too bad if you're with your best friend.
The mothers were best friends too, according to Susie. And the fathers worked together.
"We take turns on dishes and cooking," Susie said. "My mother

and I do it one meal, Tamie's mother and she do it the next."

Evidently the boys and men took turns gathering wood, hauling water, making the fire, lighting the camp stove.

The camp was remarkably quiet. No motorbikes or radios. Thank goodness.

In one camp Mel and I stayed in the radio was going full blast from morning to night, and a boy roared back and forth on a motorbike all day. It would have been tolerable if he had gone someplace, but he just roared back and forth on a dirt road in front of the tents.

But *this* was a quiet group. Just children and dog sounds. A huge campfire at night. Maybe with good friends you don't need radios and motorbikes.

But I think there is something else connected with the success of such an expedition—besides good friends and even the promise of huckleberry pies next winter.

Courage, for instance. If this expedition started five years ago, it means the children were very small. Mommie and daddy were camping out with some very tiny tots. It takes courage to pack diapers for a four-day stay in the wilderness, to wash dishes in a dishpan, carry water from the creek. And how about cooking three meals a day and picking berries while watching little children with a tempting creek nearby?

Maybe the secret is hard work. It takes hard work to organize an expedition five years in a row and make it fun so everyone is still there the fifth year.

Potluck In the Rites Of Life

Potluck Wedding, the invitation said.

I wrote right back, *Good for you. I approve. I heartily approve.* This is the second potluck wedding invitation Mel and I have received.

I wonder if it's just the younger generations who are trying this route. The two invitations we received came from the niece-nephew group.

But what a marvelous idea. Look how this would have solved the problem presented in a *Dear Abby* column. Christmas Bride wrote:

Abby, I'm in total panic. She had mailed out invitations and 14 single people answered that they were bringing a guest. Several married couples indicated they had to bring their children.

Due to space limitations and a tight budget, the bride wrote, *I cannot accommodate any more than I have already invited.*

Mel's nephew in Idaho and my nephew in Washington solved the problem wisely, politely, and, I think, graciously. They simply put right on the invitation, *Potluck lunch follows ceremony. Everyone invited.*

The ceremony took place in a church, but the reception was held, in one case, out on the lawn, and in another, in a large hall.

Why should receptions be held in restaurants or in any formal seating arrangement? That's fine if you can handle extra people without breaking your budget, but often guests would be happier with simpler arrangements and an informal air. Then if your cousin Millie drops in unexpectedly the day before the wedding—well, you bring her along.

People generally don't mind bringing a dish to a potluck. I know that a potluck wedding might sound like the end—THE END—for some people. Something left over from the hippie, flower-children era.

But I don't think so. I think it is a welcome idea for the present and future. Like potluck Thanksgiving and Christmas get-togethers. With so many women working full time, it's becoming a SuperMom *tour de force* for one person to cook a traditional holiday feast.

For years I've been saying just put a card on your front door:

> *Have floor,*
> *will share.*

I mean that a potluck is a way for someone with a rather bare house and larder to still be able to share a holiday.

The meal doesn't have to be roast beef or turkey with all the trimmings. It can be "Bread and Spread" or baked beans or pizza. The real food is the sharing, the warmth and the fellowship.

Isn't there a saying, "You can eat at home. You go out to dine." Well, on holidays you go out to be together, to share a ritual, a rite. Maybe you pray a little, offer grace, hold hands. Maybe you sing, play the guitar.

You have to observe the rituals and rites of life. Weddings and holiday celebrations are important. So don't let money or lack of money stand in the way. Just say:

> *I have the spot,*
> *You bring the pot.*

Bring an Aphorism to Dinner

This is a game for a long weekend or when you're marooned by a snowstorm. That happened to Mel and me. We were house guests at Echo Lake, and after feasting, snowshoeing, skiing and talking over the events of the year, we were sitting in front of the fire, calm and content.

I don't know who thought up the idea, but somebody said, "Why don't we all come to dinner tonight with an aphorism?"

"What's an aphorism?" 8-year-old Douglas asked.

"It's a saying or a quotation," we said. "You have to come to dinner with a quotation."

"Like 'The early bird catches the worm'?" Douglas asked.

"Fine," we said. The rules we devised were that the quotation had to lead to discussion. You couldn't just drop a clunk of lead.

I think the idea came to us because most of the group had lived abroad in the days when there was no TV, so the art of conversation was alive and well. If you were invited to a dinner, you were supposed to show up with some wit and vivacity.

But you know how that can turn out—one person has all the wit and vivacity, and the rest are the audience. This game we invented during a snowstorm at Echo Lake takes care of that danger because everybody has a turn. Everybody has his/her three minutes clear and unobstructed.

What amazed me was that the idea took off like a rocket. I didn't expect the younger folks to go along at all. Suddenly the TV clicked off. "We have to prepare," 12-year-old Lisa said.

The rest of the afternoon was like a theater: "Where's the book on quotations?" "Where's Shakespeare?" "Can I use *Puddinhead Wilson?*"

The best line of the day came from 7-year-old Jason, stomping through the living room, saying with great indignation, "Someone confiscated my aphorism."

The surprise I had during dinner was that the best topics, the ones that led to really good discussions, were brought up by the quietest people, the ones who ordinarily said not a word during meals.

Another surprise was how much discussion started with a simple quotation and ended with a kind of heart-to-heart between mother and daughter, father and son, or vice versa.

It was almost as if the teenagers said, "Hey, here's my chance—while guests are present and someone might take my side."

The teenagers brought up really controversial subjects. No wonder they were working like bees all afternoon. They had to find a quotation to fit what they wanted to talk about.

10-year-old Marty wrote a poem, an original poem. Everyone just sat and looked at him when he finished reading it. It was good and no one had ever thought of him that way. He had ideas in that poem he would never have brought out in ordinary conversation.

If you want to try this game, you have to set up firm rules. You need a clock so no one takes up more than his/her share of time. You need silence and respect for the person who has the floor.

You need guests so the family can't bog down in the usual rhubarbs. Maybe a guest has to be the master of ceremonies.

If things heat up too much, you can always go ice-skating by moonlight.

Marriage

You have to make it.
Like a cake
you have to bake it.

Jonah and the Whale Reversed

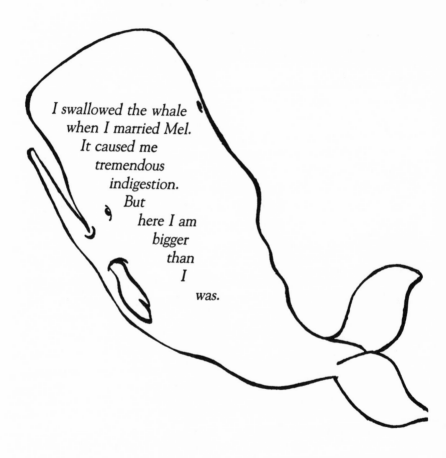

*I swallowed the whale
when I married Mel.
It caused me
tremendous
indigestion.
But
here I am
bigger
than
I
was.*

Polly, I Can
Finish the Play Now

Polly, remember the play I wrote in Chile where you got drunk and stood on the table and said, "What the hell am I going to do for the next 40 years?"

You'd just turned 40. You'd been drinking all through the bridge game. It was the best line of the play. Maybe it was the only line. Because the play never really worked. It didn't have an end. Now I know why, Polly. We hadn't lived it yet.

In the play you were thinking that your solution was to have another baby. "When I'm pregnant," you said, "is the only time I don't have this nagging inside of me—what am I going to do with my life?"

In the play I—my character, who was sort of dumb and had symptoms—said, "Polly talks like that because she went to Bryn Mawr." Now of course, after Betty Friedan and everything else, we know what was going on. Then we didn't. We were all living the American Dream, weren't we? Buying clothes on Fifth Avenue, swimming at the Country Club. We all had maids and gardeners. Our husbands had Good Jobs.

We were so lucky, we said. We played bridge—Oh, those bridge games!—10:30 a.m. to 6:30 p.m. Then the men would come to pick us up and the cocktails would start. We'd all stagger home at 9, the maid would have the children in bed, and the cook would have dinner on the table.

Why weren't we all ecstatic? The honest truth is we didn't know. Imagine that—a whole generation of women going to Bryn Mawr, Cornell University, University of California, and we didn't know.

You drank. I got symptoms. Leslie did or did not have small, discreet affairs. Marian was president of the Women's Club, 250 strong.

We didn't know how to end our play.

"A man is an instrument." That's what my housekeeper, that wise Lucy, said when I asked her why she was going to marry a man 20 years younger than she and a jailbird to boot.

In South America in those days a woman was a nobody. "A man always signs the papers," Lucy said. "The officials ask when they come to look at my property: *Where's the man of the house?*" (Lucy on her meager pay was buying a lot on the edge of the city. The sale might have been legal, and it might not have been.)

"Lucy, don't you dare sign over that property!" I screamed at least once a day. "That young man of yours will have a girlfriend and if you don't have the property in your name, you'll be out, out, OUT!"

I have 10 rules for marriage, Polly. Rule #1 is "Never mind a room of your own. You need MONEY of your own."

Isn't it funny, Polly—a man for us was the same as for Lucy—he was an instrument. Back in the '40s when you married and in the '50s when I married, the ring on our finger was the key to the life women wanted.

Was it Barbara Stanwyck or Joan Crawford who made a movie where she was a famous editor of a big women's magazine but she was not HAPPY. A military colonel seduced her on a divingboard and—fade out, fade in—goodbye magazine. Lady editor gets ring; she is now HAPPY. She is in the magic circle of warm, protected women. Our mothers sighed: "My daughter is now happily married. I can relax." Man was the instrument.

So where did we go wrong, Polly? Did we want to reverse the magic circle—jump backward off the divingboard into the lady editorship of that magazine?

Of course that's exactly what we wanted, but we didn't know it. No. We wanted both. We wanted it *all,* as they say today.

Remember the shock waves that went through the Country Club-Bridge Club-Women's Club when Dot left her husband and two children to return to the USA to get her Master's degree in geography at the University of Wisconsin? Nobody could understand it. I played tennis with her husband after she left. You talked highbrow stuff with him. Leslie invited him to dinner. He was always the available male.

Dot tried to explain to us. Her father, mother, sister, brother all had titles. They were DEFINED.

We snickered. For a Master's in geography she's jeopardizing ALL? We were ready with the axiom:

> *Wife she go for Master's degree,*
> *mistress come glad-a-lee.*

or

Graduate School: First Step to Divorce

Well, it was for you, Polly. Instead of having a baby you opted for grad school in library science. Now you're divorced. You're a librarian and you have a lover. There is the ending for the play I couldn't write because we hadn't lived it.

Leslie had one affair too many. She actually left her State Department husband for a sheik. He said he was a sheik. She actually went to some country in Arabia—just like in *The Arabian Nights.* "Are you going to live in a harem?" we asked. "Silly," she said.

She did go, but of course it was the old sadder-but-wiser, down-the-primrose-path morality bit. The State Department had to rescue her—right out of a harem. Well, it *was* an adventure.

Imagine! With all our Country Club-Bridge Club-Women's Club, Cocktail-party-dresses-you-fell-out-of, glass-slipper embassy balls, we were still ready to fly off to *The Desert Song.*

But of course it was logical. My God! that was the logical end for my play. Why didn't I see that? Oh, how dumb I was. But it hadn't happened then.

Polly, I'm going to drag out my play and write this new ending. No. It's gone past its day. Nobody would buy that today.

Marian's ending is quite logical too. Her husband's company transferred them to Dallas, and she's selling real estate like mad.

She's one of those million-dollar salespeople. Sell a million bucks, go to Hawaii. She took to it like a duck to water—straight from Country Club-Bridge Club-Women's Club teas. Well, it's the same really, Marian says. She owns five houses, all over the world. Her husband is now retired, the children grown up. That's a good ending for my play.

And my life? Well, I'm here. And Mel's here. Rule #2 for marriage: Liberate him first. I liberated Mel from work. When he came home one day from his office and said, "I pulled the plug," which in miners' language means, "I quit." I didn't jump up and down and say, "Oh God! what will become of us!" I didn't faint and moan low. I didn't say anything. Probably I was in shock.

I had to tell my friends of the Country Club-Bridge Club-Women's Club. "He has every right in the world," I said. "We won't starve. We don't have children. What do we need a lot of money for?"

Polly, you astute observer—you said, "Methinks the lady doth protest too much." Bryn Mawr sagacity of course.

Was it coincidence—what else could it be—but I fell into a job that same month exactly. All by serendipity—if I understand the word. To me it means you are heading for somewhere—you don't get there—but you land at a place that turns out just as good, maybe even better.

That was when I interviewed Miss Grey about her newly in-augurated summer school and got so enthusiastic about it over watercress sandwiches and Twining's Lapsang Souchong tea imported from London that a week later when Miss Grey called up and asked if I would like to teach Introduction to Comparative Religions I said—even though I felt a little faint—"Certainly."

That was the first job where I got a paycheck since 1952, when Mel and I left New York.

So I liberated Mel, or he liberated himself, and then I was free to do the same. At least that's what happened. Mel retired to hunt and fish right there in the Andes Mountains, and I retired from being the woman behind the man behind the desk.

I couldn't even wait dinner for my dear hubby any more now. Up to then I and the dinner had sat together in the warming oven. Mel was a business rep. Business reps do business quite often outside the office. All wives know the phone calls that say, "I'm on my way," then 30 minutes later—again, "I'm on my way."

"I don't mind," I said to myself. "I am warm, protected, loved, cherished, cared for—and I play tennis at the Country Club. The least I can do is wait dinner for the breadwinner of the family."

When I went from teaching at Santiago College (which was a secondary school) to teaching at the Catholic University of Chile, the hours were later: 2 to 4 and 5 to 7. That's when I liberated the dinner hour. "Don't wait for me," I said. "Have your dinner when you want it. Lucy will serve you."

Of course the house went to pot. I didn't see the dust in the corners. Lucy didn't either. She was more near-sighted than I.

Now Mel and I are back in the USA. He is still hunting and fishing. I am still teaching. The dust is still in the corners. Maybe it's the same dust.

10 Rules for Marriage

I admit these 10 rules are from a woman's point of view. Men, do you mind? I hope you'll write a set of your own.

1) Virginia Woolf said you need a room of your own. I say never mind a room of your own. You need money of your own. It doesn't have to be much—just enough to be able to, well, leave home, I guess. A person may have no intention of leaving home, but you need the feeling you could.

2) Liberate him first. When Mel retired early, he liberated himself from the Macho Male role of The Great Provider, and I liberated myself from being the woman behind the man. We live on less, but we are both free. Either one can mess up the kitchen; either one can go fishing; either one can watch football. And each one has to clean the bathroom.

3) Don't divorce at first twinge. The second marriage will be full of holes too.

4) Adjust a little, but not like a doormat. Doormats are made to be walked on.

5) If he breaks your arm, shoot him. No, don't do that, but leave him flat. Allow those genes to die out.

6) Don't read women's magazines. They are a trap. They lead to Barefoot and Pregnant, *P* for Perfection, and SuperMom.

7) Barefoot and Pregnant is the original trap. Don't relive it. Have children when and if you want them. And if you can love them. Face it—some people are not mothers.

8) *P* for Perfection is taking the place of Barefoot and Pregnant. Perfect house, perfect meals, perfect children, perfect party on Saturday night. Don't do it.

9) SuperMom is nuts. Don't let anyone con you into that role.

10) At 9 p.m. say to your spouse, "Hey, did I make you laugh today? Did you make me laugh today? Well, now's the time."

10 Rules When Contemplating Marriage

1) Don't marry for mad sex. Have it first. But ask yourself: "Am I a sex goddess? Can I handle it?"

2) Don't marry young. 30 is a good age. Of course, the Fresh Young Faces will be taken by then. Or *they'll* be looking for Fresh Young Faces.

3) Before marrying a HUNK, ask yourself: "When love leaves, as it might well do, what will I have?"

4) Before marrying the Sweet Lovable Ne'er-do-well, ask yourself: "Can I support him without reminding him every two minutes?"

5) Before marrying Peter Pan, ask yourself: "Will he clean the bathroom?"

6) Before marrying Mr. Macho Male, ask yourself: "Does he want a doll that he can carry? Do I want to be a doll?"

7) Now I am addressing the masculine sex: Men, don't be the strong, silent type while the maneuvering goes on. Before you know it, your wagon will be hitched to the wrong star. Just write True or False in front of the following items and then present the list to your Intended:

a. I really do want a doll that I can carry.

b. I want my wife home before me in the evening.

c. I don't want a woman who earns more than I do.

d. I want a big family.

e. I'll help around the house of course but housework really is a woman's job.

(Add as many more to the list as you feel strong about.)

8) Men: if a group—a gaggle—a gathering—of females is spending the evening at your Intended's apartment, what term would you use to ask the following question: "Have the _____ left yet?" Pick one:

a. Ladies
b. Women
c. Girls
d. Gals
e. Dolls
f. Broads

This item may sound frivolous, but it may also be like the canary in the mine. Either you and your Intended are at the same stage of evolution or you are not.

9) Who's going to cook? Who's going to have the babies? If the husband has a wife, can the wife have a wife? Who will solace whom?

These are not questions to ask; these are things to feel right about.

10) Men and women both: Walk with cheer. There *are* marriages "made in heaven." There *is* love "til death do us part." People *do* meet each other. I met Mel "some enchanted evening across a crowded room" when he was 40 and I was 27.

Sex

Sex won't cure warts. You'd think it did the way it's touted nowadays. Even by psychiatrists. Instead of being on the couch, you're in bed.

I'm not saying this is wrong. What I'm saying is that sex is not the panacea for all the woes of the world.

> *It's fine, it's good,*
> *but you still have to get up*
> *in the morning,*
> *and what are you going to do*
> *with the day?*

Hi, Elizabeth—You Did OK

Elizabeth the First, Queen of England,
how many people asked you
if you were a Virgin Queen?
You spit in their eye — I know you did.
"Off with their heads!" you ordered.

I don't care if you were a virgin or not.
You did better than that.
You kept your head. You kept your throne.
You held the reins 45 years.

Knights and nobles,
kings and courtiers —
you played them like an organ.

Did you laugh at night —
a sheer shudder,
exquisite —
of power?

For you, my queen, sex could have been a trap.
It's meant to be. For both men and women.
It's the bait to perpetuate the species.
Fine. Very necessary. But KNOW IT.

Advice for Lovers

Even though no one tells the truth about sex—it may be the purest, truest, most genuine "Emperor's New Clothes" story ever told—nevertheless:

Make Love, Not War

What else can men and women do together as easily, as unencumbered, as inexpensively, as this?

But Learn How

Maybe we should teach, not just sex education, but SEX PRACTICE.
Oh me, oh my—did I say *THAT?*

Alexa

I do not deal in love;
The word is too big for the page

"They were so perfect for each other," Alexa's mother said. "He calm; she hot-blooded, passionate. Alexa came home from the honeymoon glowing. Ten months later a baby, and still the honeymoon goes on."

I, living across the street, had to take this with a grain of salt. Every morning when the young husband came out of the house to get into his car to go to work, there right behind him, in her robe, was Alexa screaming like a fishwife.

I got even more of the true picture when Lucy's niece Leonta went to work for Alexa. Leonta didn't last a week. Alexa threw her out bodily. "The devil is in her," Leonta said.

Alexa was hot-tempered before she was married and she was hot-tempered after she was married. Sex didn't cure that.

It didn't even cure the hot-bloodedness. Alexa took a lover.

Lucy reported this to me. Because Lucy was a sort of philosopher people confided in her. "Love is like a cold," Alexa told Lucy. "The fever burns, then it goes away."

About 10 years later when I visited Santiago, I walked down our old street. There was an apartment house where Alexa's chalet had been. "What happened to Alexa?" I asked the only person I knew who still lived on that street—my English friend Maggie.

"She's still married to Jorge."

"I can't believe it," I said.

"For the sake of the children," Maggie said.

Is this a purely Latin idea? Lovers come and go, but the children stay. They stay with the house. Like cats do. People can leave a house, you know, but the cat can stay. It will adopt the new owners.

(My friend Carol bought a bookshop called Sidney's. Sidney was the cat. It went with the shop. It has adopted Carol and lives very happily at the shop—night and day. If Carol sells the shop, Sidney will stay.)

Alexa has three children. They are growing up with Alexa and Jorge. Alexa is still hot-tempered and hot-blooded. She still screams at Jorge in her robe. She still has lovers. He may or may not have a mistress. I don't know his side of the story.

Like Sidney the cat, the house is there; the family is there; the children are there. Love? Love is like a cold. The fever burns then it goes.

Cinderella, did you make any friends after you found your prince? Were the two of you ALL to each other? The bells rang, the earth moved, (Hemingway said that in *For Whom the Bell Tolls*) and after that? But of course, Cinderella, everyone knows you lived *happily ever after.*

Teenagers, You *Can* Say No

It is better to marry than to burn, the Bible says. In a way, this is what the smart, young advice-givers are saying to teenagers today. "You *can* say no," they're saying to the young girls. "You will not be ostracized."

We can also speak to the young men:

> *You will not die*
> *or go blind*
> *or blow up.*

In fact, this may be an opportunity.

> *If your hormones are sizzling*
> *use that energy*
> *to catapult yourself*
> *OUT of your cellar*
> *into the SUN.*
>
> *In what field do you wish to shine*
> *like a 200-watt bulb, my son?*
> *SEX?*
> *Any rabbit can out-perform you there*
> *How about LIFE?*

Aging

Remember the thesis I nailed to the door of the Senior Citizen Center? It belongs right here, and I've added three lines:

> *Throw out that 10-cent coffee.*
> *Charge us 40 cents*
> *but give free herb tea.*
> *Don't natter on with drug seminars.*
> *We know we have arthritis.*
> *Give us something bigger than arthritis.*
> *WE WISH TO BE INVOLVED, TO SEEK, TO QUEST,*
> *TO ADVENTURE, TO LAUGH AT DEATH.*
> *"LET IT COME! I HAVE LIVED!"*

We Study Grizzly Adams

"There he is—study him," I said to the Gerontology conference. "He'll snowshoe right through that door."

I was joking, but I *was* expecting Mel. I was giving a talk to the first annual meeting of the Montana Gerontology Society. Mel dropped me off at the hotel in Great Falls where the meeting was, then he drove on to Pishkun Reservoir to fish.

This was in May 1983. Would you expect a blizzard on May 9? That's what happened. I looked out of the window while I was talking and snow was gusting, blowing and pelting. There had been red tulips outside the hotel—in bloom. Now they were in a snowbank.

"I hope my husband gets here," I said.

"The roads are closed," the conference director said.

That's when I said, "Well, he'll snowshoe right through that door."

Actually he made it in his car. Just barely. Not knowing the roads were closed, he came on through, inching his way along in the white-out.

He blew in the door of the hotel, sleet-and-snow-covered. "Grizzly Adams!" the conference said. "Welcome, pardner!"

"Well," I said, "that's what Gerontology is all about, isn't it—how to keep people *doing* instead of *being done to.*"

She Walked the Arthritis Right Out of Her Knees

Katie Argo is now 75. She was 60 when she took up hiking. At first she couldn't even walk four blocks. "I had arthritis so bad my knees were all swollen," Katie recounts. "I could hardly move. I said to myself, I have to do something. I don't want to just get worse.

"I made some real changes in my life. I took up hiking. Well, at first I just took up walking—and just barely that. The first day I walked around the block, my knees hurt so much I didn't know if I could keep on with my idea. But I said to myself, I have to do it. The next day I walked around the block again and it hurt less instead of more, so I kept on going, a little farther every day.

"Then I met Vernie Linn in my garden club, and we started walking together. After a while we called it hiking because we were walking five miles every day, and we were climbing hills. Then I heard about the Women on Wednesday hiking group. At first I went on just the short hikes. Six miles round trip. But now I do them all. 10 and 12 miles round trip. And you remember that 18-mile round trip?"

"Don't remind me," I said.

"It's been every Wednesday—rain or shine. I'm now 75 years old."

"Did you change anything else in your life, Katie?" I asked.

"Yes. I changed my diet. I eat only two real meals a day now, and a lot less meat. I think I eat meat only when I go out. And I gave up coffee. Well, not 100%. I drink coffee every Sunday when I go out with a group of friends for Sunday brunch."

"Are you high all day?" I asked.

"Yes," she said. "I'm high all day."

"Well, we can't be perfect," I said.

"I also gave up sugar," Katie added. "I don't bake at home, and I don't put sugar in my tea or on my cereal. I don't eat desserts."

"So you changed your whole way of living." I said.

"I don't miss the old way at all," Katie said. "I feel so much better now."

Trade Your Senior Citizen Card for a Student I.D.

"Wouldn't you rather have a student I.D.?"
That's what I say to the Senior Citizens.
Colleges are wide open these days.
You can wear your polyester, keep
your bifocals on your nose, pop pills,
drink Geritol—and speak up.

I had to become a perennial student because I needed the I.D. card. Without a driver's license (I don't drive), without credit cards (I don't have any), did I exist?

"I want to walk across the oval and belong," I wrote. "I need a home away from home." That's what the magazine *Psychology Today* said. People need a hangout. Not your workplace, not your home. You need a third place. The university is my third place.

I did what Thomas Wolfe said you couldn't do—I've gone home again. I'm right back where I started from:

Student
Beatnik
Career Woman
Wife
Drone
Teacher
Professor
Repatriate
Retired Couple
Student

Look at that—10 again. Does one's mind run in 10s? Does it have to do with the moon and the tides?

I'll find out at the university. That's what I'm there for. Not to get a job—but to seek wisdom. I take courses in philosophy. Why not? Do I want to go dumb to my grave?

I said that during a talk to the University Career Services. I said we have to go to every Senior Citizen Center and say to the elders: "How would you like to trade your Senior Citizen card for a student I.D.?"

Mad as a hatter? Not at all. What are we going to do with our long, long life? We don't just fade away at 50 or 60 or 70. We take vitamins, we EAT RIGHT, we're alive, we're buzzing. I said straight out to the Senior Citizens: "Do you want to go dumb to your grave?"

I told the Gerontology conference (I have nothing to lose. Nobody pays me.) "Don't build an empire. If Gerontology becomes a business, then won't it be your business to increase the business?"

What did the British say about the Yanks in World War II? *Overfed, Oversexed and Over Here.* If we don't watch out, Gerontology will go just like that. For a favored few it will be:

Over-insured,
Over-hospitalized,
Over-technologized.

Won't those favored few feel like saying—

Don't speak to me about that woman
with 13 children.
I can't be responsible. I'm 70 years old.
I deserve my rest. I deserve the best.
I'll speak to my Congressman.

"Are we playing a gimmee game between the young and the old?" I said to the Gerontology conference.

Being a student is the opposite of young versus old. It is you and me together—it is we, us. If you're throwing pots in an art class, it doesn't matter what age you are. You talk, you visit, you go to art shows. You wear jeans with patched knees.

And you're OPEN TO OPPORTUNITY.

I got on National Public Radio because I was a student. I was taking a course in Radio-TV and my advisor said, "What can you do for your project?"

I said, "I know a lot about edible wild plants. I could do a chat once a week."

I'm still doing it. "This is Kim Williams with her once-a-week chat on edible wild plants and related topics." It's mostly related topics by now. Well, a person grows, spreads out.

My advisor sent a tape of my chitchats to NPR in Washington, D.C. and somebody there said OK.

Serendipity. Pure. But of course I wasn't sitting home watching TV. I say to the Senior Citizens, "You're too young to die. Nothing will happen to you if you're glued to that 10-cent coffee. You have to look for a door that is open a crack and then put your eyeball through."

I don't know what all will happen to me next. I have my Master's degree—it took me six years—but I'm still taking classes. I wore out two I.D. cards already.

Fun is overrated.
Travel is overrated.

I had a roommate on my trip to Hong Kong (I had to smell Hong Kong before I died) and she told me this was her sixth trip. "You ought to endow an orphanage," I said.

I think Senior Citizens travel so much not because they are having so much FUN, but because there's nothing more attractive to do. George Burns said golf is fun only when you have to *sneak out* to do it. Mr. Burns is still working, and he's in his 80s.

Pablo Jury, a South American friend of ours, said, "The young talk about sex. The middle-aged talk about business. The old talk about their operations."

Eunice Brown, you have it right: "Don't tell me how you are, and I won't tell you how I am."

Eunice, you gave us the best laugh of the day at the Gerontology conference. I used your idea in my talk. I said, "It can take up a lot of your time if you tell each of your friends how you are and then they tell you how they are."

Suddenly a woman in the back row, without raising her hand or anything, said good and loud, "It not only could! It does!"

Then I told them about your flitting around in the graveyard. "Let's go to the cemetery," Eunice said to me one day quite shortly after Mel and I moved across the street from her.

"Are we going to rob a grave?" I asked. Eunice loves funny remarks. She'll laugh a good loud snort and even give you a hug.

"We're not going to rob a grave," Eunice said. "The caretaker saves the plastic flowers for me. I need them to make my Easter trees."

Eunice cleared $800 for the Handicapped Children's Association that spring, just from making and selling these homemade Easter "trees." The "trees" were made out of baubles and beads and bits of fluff—even old jewelry—all glued on to a lilac-branch skeleton and covered with the plastic flowers from the cemetery. They were three-dimensional works of art, and people bought them as fast as Eunice and her crew of helpers made them.

This crew of helpers illustrates another of Eunice's ideas—doing things *with people*. She had her house full of people working, talking, laughing.

And the money was a bridge connecting the old to the young. This is one of Eunice's basic tenets. The day after she went to the Friends of Youth banquet with her ribs strapped and her leg black and blue, she came over to tell me about the event. "People were surprised to see me. They had read about the accident in the paper."

"You had a brush with eternity," I said sternly.

Eunice refused to get serious. "I'm going to come back as a teen-age missionary," she said.

"That's your reincarnation?" I asked.

"I don't know about reincarnation, but I can't spend much time in heaven. There's too much to do here." Eunice became serious now. "I think we have to do more for the young," she said. "Just as the Senior Citizens have centers to hang out at, the young need places to hang out at—have fun, make friends. And they need jobs. A teenager who has never had a job will never catch up."

No wonder, Eunice, on your 88th birthday an ad appeared in the *Missoulian:*

HERE IS A STORY ABOUT A GREAT, GREAT PERSON

It was quite a long piece. It told how you were born on a farm and harnessed horses and plowed roads—and you were never more than five feet tall. You rode a horse to school, became a schoolteacher, taught at a business college, had a novelty shop, learned to appraise antiques. (You were also a wife, Eunice, and I know you took care of several people in your family who were in wheelchairs.)

The ad ended: *Ya still don't know who Montana's sweetheart is? Well, it's Eunice Brown—that's who.*

I have something else to add to my thesis for the door of the Senior Citizen Center:

> *Nail a picture of Eleanor Roosevelt*
> *to the wall.*
> *Embroider on the bottom:*
> *"We must be up and doing."*
> *Eleanor did did did all over the world,*
> *to the day she died.*

When I joined Jewel Goakes' Workshop of the Arts in Santiago, Chile, and we adopted the resolution: "During meetings you will not talk about maids, husbands, babies, prices and going home to the USA," we did relent just a little for our tea-table discussions. We said, "You may read books and discuss them."

I once had to discuss existentialism. "That will stretch your brains," Polly said to me.

It did. I came to the tea table with a motto: "I wish to pare my life to its essentials." But of course I didn't know what the essentials were.

I was still worrying about the moon in my fingernails. Can you imagine—I actually worried about the shape of the moon and the cuticle in my 10 fingernails. Once, in a hotel, I couldn't go down to eat with my husband until I went to the lobby and bought a bottle of nail polish of the exact same shade as my lipstick.

If nothing else, dear Senior Citizens, you are using your tax money when you become a student. Turn down the heat in your house and go study in the library. Carry a load of books and say, "I belong!"

Fern Bonnell's Private Volunteer Program

My swimming companion, Fern Bonnell, said to me when she was 81, "I have joined the Senior Citizen volunteer program."

"Oh," I said. "I thought you didn't want to drive your car in the winter so you had decided not to join the volunteer program."

"I have my own volunteer program," she answered.

"Your own?"

"Yes. I said to myself if other people are going off to kindergartens or hospitals to help—well, there's a group right under my nose and why don't I help them? They're in my own apartment house. I don't have to take my car out and drive. I don't have to be picked up and dropped off. I am doing my volunteer work right in my own apartment house."

"What are you doing?"

"Well, you know I enjoy housekeeping. All those years when I was a teacher I didn't get much chance to housekeep. I gave everything a lick and a promise. Well, now I am retired and I have lots of time. My apartment is small and doesn't keep me busy. I read and I swim, but I still have free time.

"Now—in my apartment building, right across the hall—there are three young men. They're students, and they're very nice. I've known them for two years. I bake them a pie or cake once in a while and they take me out to dinner once in a while—like Thanksgiving, for instance.

"Well, I've noticed that they like to cook, but they don't get around to cleaning up the kitchen. The dishes pile up.

"So I said to them, may I be your Senior Citizen volunteer? I'll come over three times a week and clean up your kitchen. You can't pay me and you don't have to do anything for me. I want to do it because I have free time and I don't want to read all day or watch TV. I never turn on the TV until the news at 5:00.

"The boys said, 'Fine, you can do that if you really want to.' "

"I go in at noon when they're all out and wash the dishes and mop the floor. I don't do the livingroom or the bedrooms—just the kitchen. It gives me pleasure because I like to see the clean dishes all stacked up. I like to see the pots shining and the floor freshly mopped."

"But you don't get a medal this way," I said. "Nobody puts your name on a list and calls it out at a meeting."

Fern smiled. "Here's my name on a list," she said. She showed me a card signed by Charles, Richard and Robert.

10 Rules for Growing Old Gracefully

1) Write your epitaph once a year. It gives you perspective on where you've been and where you're going. Don't be afraid of death. Look it in the eye and say:

> *Let it come.*
> *I have lived.*

2) Don't let people stuff you with cheap sugary food and cheap fried food. Buy your clothes at the Goodwill shop and eat fresh vegetables. Don't say, "I can't cook for one." You can.

3) If you join the Senior Citizen Center, run the place. Put a sign on your mirror: *Wear out! Don't rust out!*

4) Mix with another generation at least once a week. If you find yourself talking about the past, quickly switch to the future tense.

5) Start an "Exclaim and Admire" Club. Hand out cards saying,

> *Did you exclaim about something today?*
> *Did you admire something today?*

6) Holler instead of complaining. Whining, griping, complaining aren't half as useful as a HUGE FAT HOLLER, the kind where you GET MAD and then DO SOMETHING. Say, "This is my project. I will put time and effort into this. I will fight. I will fight to the finish." Your finish? Maybe that too, but don't we all want to die with our boots on?

7) Make an exercise resolution. "I am not too old to exercise. Gently maybe, but I'll do it. I may even work up a sweat." A GLOW, ladies.

8) Make a leave-home resolution. "I will leave home and come back. Once a day I will walk out of my abode and stay out for two hours. I will walk in the weather."

9) Make a share-your-home resolution. "I will think seriously of living with another person instead of living alone. I will not make the statement, *I can't live with anyone.*"

10) Make a keep-your-brain-alive resolution. "I will not let my brain atrophy. I will:

    a) Take a course
    b) Teach a course
    c) Tutor a student
    d) Play duplicate bridge
    e) Run for political office."

Death

*Don't go ahead of time
And don't go ignominiously*

I Wish To Die in Peace, Not in Pieces

"I have to write three more books," I said one day on my local radio program, "then I'll jump into the Clark Fork River."

"Don't do that," a lady wrote in panic. "Call me. Let's talk. Even if you are terminally ill don't do that."

So we got into a discussion about death, the proper way to go. I quoted a poem I once wrote:

> *I do not want your heart,*
> *nor liver, nor kidney*
> *nor brain.*
> *I would not linger*
> *merely to lengthen*
> *a span that is already spent.*

"Ah," the lady said, "but how does one know when it's spent?"

Oh for the old days when one believed that Death came for one and that was that. Like the Spanish story where Death came into the cafe. "Ah, there's the one I'm looking for—that bearded one with all that hair on his head." Death bowed to the chosen one. "I'll be back for you shortly," he said and left the cafe.

"Not for me he won't," Ricardo said. He ran to the barbershop next door and had his head and face shaved clean as a billiard ball. He was so secure in his disguise that he went back into the same cafe.

Death walked into the cafe, looked around and said, "Ah, the bearded one left. Well, no matter. I'll take old baldy here."

Of course it was Ricardo. When we believed like that, what use was a plastic—or real—heart, head, lung or kidney?

"Kim Williams, not only are you economically inactive, now you don't even want to use doctors and hospitals," Trixie said.

"They can set my broken leg," I said.

> *A hospital is like a sausage factory:*
> *it needs bodies.*
> *If it has empty beds it can't run.*
> *Send me coronaries, send me appendectomies —*
> *that's the Song of the Hospital.*
> *I am hungry, I must be fed.*
> *Without bodies the machines can't hum,*
> *the wires can't strum.*

When I thought I had the Big C (Isn't that what John Wayne called it?) I wrote another verse for Song of the Hospital.

> *Cancer is big business.*
> *Do this, do that —*
> *you will still die*
> *but we will make money*
> *and you will have hope.*
> *HOPE FOR WHAT?*
> *That we will make money*
> *and you will have hope.*

She'll Drop Dead Any Minute, But What a Way To Go

That's what Roberto said as his mother-in-law—whom the doctors pronounced on her deathbed—suddenly burst into song in the middle of her birthday party. She sang a whole song without accompaniment, without teeth, without missing a note.

And she ate roast pork and birthday cake made out of three thin layers of cake and three thick layers of whipped cream. All this on her deathbed.

Except she wasn't in bed. With a cane and leaning on her daughter or her son-in-law or her grandchildren, she maneuvered from room to room and up and down stairs.

Mel and I had just arrived in South America. I was aghast. "Should she be out of bed?" I asked. "How did the doctors allow a thing like this?"

"Nobody asked them," the daughter Juanita said calmly. "Why should Mama sit looking at four walls on her birthday and everybody going *Shhh?*"

Nobody went *Shhh* at this party. Everyone shouted at the top of his voice. There were 28 people from age 3 to 83. There were the four children of the old lady, all the 13 grandchildren, three great-grandchildren, plus neighbors. There was also a lifelong friend who was a folklore singer. She was now out of voice, but that didn't deter her at all. A guitar was sent for, the singer cracked all the high notes, but the noise and applause rang to the rafters.

This is when the old lady, the dying patient, rose up and sang—all by herself—a love song from beginning to end. She sat down looking completely happy while applause deafened the room.

And Roberto said to Mel and me, "She'll drop dead any minute but look at her. Surrounded by everyone she cares about—a party going on—noise, shouting, singing. What could be better?" He poured champagne all around and we stood up to drink a toast: "May Doña Elsa live to sing again next year."

The next day I said to Juanita, "How is your mother today? She must feel a bit under the weather."

"She feels terrible," Juanita said. "We all feel terrible. But she had a good time last night. Did you?"

"I feel honored to have been invited," I said.

I went home and said to Mel, "I still worry about grandmother. Pineapple cake with whipped cream. Champagne. And at two in the morning she got out on the floor and danced with her grandson."

Mel's answer was like Roberto's. "Well, if she's dead next year, anyway she danced this year."

I had to think about that. She had danced with her grandson who had just graduated from college. And she did this with her family, her neighbors and her friends watching.

I was reminded of a line from that old play *You Can't Take It With You*. There was a character, the Grand Duchess Olga Katrina. I once played her—in a leopard cape. One of her lines (she has only four) is, *"Ah, Kalenkhov, how we haf leeved."*

I didn't call Juanita—she would have been taking a nap—but I sent a silent wish to Doña Elsa: "Live it up, old grandmother."

With His Boots On, Yet!

It was a memorial in the middle of the Selway-Bitterroot Wilderness. Mel and I came upon it while backpacking. The sign was nailed on a tall pine tree. There was the man's name, date of birth, then these words:

> DIED HERE—Oct 1980
> In the heart of
> the mountains
> in his hunting camp
> on the back of
> his horse
> his wish was
> FULFILLED

He died with his boots on—in the most beautiful spot in the world. I can call it a beautiful spot now. I couldn't when I was there. My dear husband conned me into backpacking along a trail that wasn't a trail. With 30 or 40 pounds on our backs we had to go through a JUNGLE. There were hidden rocks and hidden holes and hidden windfalls (which are old fallen tree trunks).

I stubbed my toes; I stumbled; I fell into creeks and crevices. By the time I reached the clearing where the memorial was, I was ready to be a memorial myself: DIED HERE—August 1983 . . .

"Shhh," Mel said as I was scolding and hollering about the non-trail he had led me on, "there might be an elk right up there on that old avalanche slide."

I collapsed under the memorial pine. The ground was grassy. The view was green meadow, green forest, green mountain. It was the kind of place an elk could inhabit. The top of the avalanche slide was exactly where an elk would stand and bugle.

Ernest Hemingway, I bet your soul is in a place like this.

To the Ant Who Didn't Know How To Pray

Lucy wrote that poem and gave it to me. I was expected to critique it. "Lucy, what good would it have done that ant to pray?" I said. "A cow steps on the anthill and everything is gone."

"The ant puts it back together," Lucy said. "The ant is close to the ground. He thinks small. But this ant wanted to pray and he didn't know how. He asked the swallow. Then he asked the fox."

"Lucy, does this poem go on and on like the story of Sinbad the Sailor?"

Lucy smiled happily. I had caught on. We had gone to the Sinbad movie together. If life is not an *AVENTURA,* what is it?

Lucy died of cancer, five years after Mel and I left Chile. Her husband Segundo (he told me later) served her "her last cup of hot water."
She'd always said to me, "When you die, you need someone to bring you (serve you) your last cup of hot water."

Lucy, at least I read your poem. We read it together.

The Light Does Not Go Out

It was probably a silly thing to do—to fire the doctor—but I saw things going too fast, out of my control. I've seen that happen. A friend said to me, "My aunt didn't want any of that (the hooked-up-to-machines part), but suddenly there she was. She was even sent to a hospital out of state. We followed her from one place to another. She didn't even know us."

I was scared to take that first step. Once you're lying in a hospital bed—in that half of a gown—you're only something that things are done to. You're a blob of protoplasm with an umbilical cord fastened to Lord-knows-what.

What kind of a battle with death can a blob of protoplasm wage? It's outside forces entirely that wage the battle, and you are the battleground.

"No!" I said. "I must wage my battle first. I must contend with death. If I lose, I'll hie me to Singapore to the Street of the Dead: To die in peace, not in pieces."

When I was in Singapore, I visited the Street of the Dead. People went there to die. They lay on small cots inside a large building. Outside in the street their families kept the watch. The men played mah jongg; the women sewed; the children ran back and forth. There was life and there was death.

I think a good hospice is the modern equivalent of Singapore's Street of the Dead.

I also think one shouldn't wait for a cancer scare to come to terms with death. One should live so that when death approaches one can say, "Well, I have lived." Or better—like the Grand Duchess Olga Katrina: *"Ah, Kalenkhov, how we haf leeved."*

Maybe we need a new myth—to live by and to die by.

"Bye, Bill. Our spirits will meet in another realm," I said to a friend who died. I mean I wrote that in a letter. I didn't send the letter, but I wrote it.

I meant our energy goes somewhere. His energy will and my energy will. They might very well meet.

The energy might not be in the same form. I could be a treefrog, talking all the time, at home in water and on land, sitting on a lilypad by moonlight. That life could be OK. Oh, I know there are night-flying bats that eat treefrogs. Well, everything gets eaten sooner or later. Death is a change.

Hi, Bill. Hi, Hemingway. Hi, Pop—you came from Hungary; you came a long way. Eunice, you and I will meet. Shall we haunt someone? No. Let's make Easter trees in some perpetual graveyard.

Religion, God & Gods

Of course God exists.
A hawk flies.
A whale swims.
Clouds move.
I choose.

I believe in God.
I believe in gods.
You know how a movie
can fade in and fade out?
I can fade into a tree,
a tree can fade into a mountain,
a mountain can fade into the sky.
And God is above ALL.

If Religion Helps You Any Way at All, GO TO IT!

I have religion in my bones
although I cannot explain it
or understand it.
I accept the universe and my life.
I do not accept injustice.
LORD GODS, I DO NOT ACCEPT INJUSTICE

Mom, did the Bible help you? They say religion is "the opiate of the masses." Without religion, Mom, could you have stood it? You might have left Pop and all of us seven children.

On Mom's 96th birthday I sent her a recipe for Hungarian strudel. Why did I do that? Mom's been making strudel all her life. It was because everything I saw reminded me that she was 96 and she wouldn't be here forever. I wanted to say, "Thank you for coming to America, Mom."

You were only 22, Mom. Once I asked, "Did you come steerage?" I'd read about that in a history book—ships packed with people like sardines and the ones who came steerage had their way paid but they had to work for the person who paid the fare.

Mom, you got quite huffy when I said that. "Certainly not," you said. "My family paid my way."

Still, you worked as a housekeeper, Mom, a maid for a Hungarian family in Pittsburgh. You couldn't speak English, so you worked for a Hungarian family. You made strudel and cherry soup. Just as you did for us on the farm—that terrible farm that didn't grow anything but rocks.

And children. Seven of us. And chickens and ducks and pigs and cows and sheep.

Mom, how did you do all that? Take care of seven children. Well, even have them in the first place—all at home without a doctor.

And you helped Pop (we always called our father Pop). You helped Pop build the house we lived in. You made our clothes, some of them out of flour sacks. The sheets were all out of flour sacks.

Mom, I could cry for you. But why would I do that? You're here at 96 and all seven of us children are here.

Mom, you never learned to speak English properly. I used to think that was terrible. I was in a play once in grade school and you came to see it in a horse and buggy. I didn't know whether I wanted you to come. I'm sorry, Mom, that I was so dumb. Now I wish I could speak Hungarian.

When Mel and I lived in South America, there were all kinds of Hungarian people there. They wouldn't have anything to do with me. You're a *dummkopf*, they said. *Dummkopf* is German. Maybe most Hungarians speak German, too. Anyway, *dummkopf* means *dumbhead* and that's what I was. I grew up in a Hungarian-German household, and I didn't learn anything but English. I wanted to be like the Knickerbockers. They probably came over on the Mayflower.

Now everyone is looking up their roots—their ethnic roots. Did I have a grandfather, Mom, who walked in the woods and wrote poetry? Did I have an aunt who was nearsighted and talked to birds?

Maybe I'll never know. You don't talk much about the past, Mom. That's gone, you say.

The farm is gone too. Everyone in the family is in a city or town. Were we city people, Mom? No, you said you worked on a potato farm. But you walked for an hour to get there. I think the farms in Hungary weren't where people lived. I think the people lived in villages and went out of the villages to the land.

Mom, we're trying to do that here in Montana. We want people to live in the center of the towns and leave green space outside. We want to grow potatoes and have dairy farms and fresh vegetables.

I ought to go to Hungary some day. You never went back, Mom. "Why should I?" you said. "I'm here now." Good heavens, Mom, you're a Zen person. BE HERE NOW. You don't know the word *Zen*, Mom. Well, you don't need it. You're 96 and making strudel for the firemen's ball.

Pop, We Both Swam Upstream

I was 12 years old. It was the first poem I ever wrote. It was published in the *Albany Knickerbocker News:*

> *I am only a poor wandering fool,*
> *a tramp who has never been to school.*
> *But I know more about life than you,*
> *about God and the universe too.*

I meant *a tramp who has never been to church* but I had to use *school* because of the rhyme. In those days I didn't know that you could write poems that didn't rhyme.

I never knew enough to forgive you, Pop. I fought with you to the end. I shouldn't have. You came from Hungary. How could you deal with children who WENT OFF AND BECAME AMERICANS at six years of age? But didn't we follow you, Pop? You ran away in Hungary. You left home, came to America. You swam upstream all your life, like a salmon.

> *At Cornell University*
> *I read the shelf of philosophy*
> *from one end to the other.*
> *I read the shelf of religion*
> *from one end to the other.*
> *I came out where I went in.*
> *My mind whirled.*
> *I jumped off the mountain*
> *into a lake of cold blue water.*

Pop, you subscribed us to the Albany newspaper. You paid the bill. You hitched up the horses to pick up four boxes of books the Hudson City Public Library threw out. I became those four boxes of books.

Pop, we should have understood each other.

It's OK Lucy

Lucy, you wouldn't have had to fight with the Catholic church if you'd come along a little later. There are Catholic priests now who would have married you. They would have let you come in the front door of the church.

I told you not to go to that fancy red church in our neighborhood, Lucy. "Those padres don't understand," I said. "They're accustomed to being asked to dinner by the owners of haciendas."

You joined the Pentecostal church, Lucy. They married you. Well, in a way the red-church padres did you a favor. They wouldn't marry you. That was a favor because your first boyfriend Raul was a drunk and a good-for-nothing.

Lucy and I actually talked about God and religion. I smile when I say that because I couldn't do that with my country-club circle. I'd go to dinner parties and—well, you know how dinner-party conversation goes. It did in our world down there in South America anyway. "Now, let's not talk about sex, religion or politics." A small part of my mind—unawakened though it was—had a nagging sense of disquiet. I wanted to say, "Well, what else is there worth talking about? You've cut out life and death."

But then, who wants to deal with life and death? Better to stick to golf for the men and clothes for the women.

I should have taken you by the hand, Lucy, and led you to some of the younger Catholic priests. But I didn't know any. I'd left the church—all churches. I was studying religion like a course in college. I was dissecting it like a frog.

The Pentecostal church group held out their hand to you, Lucy. People got up in meetings and spoke. They said what was in their heart and soul. "I want to stop drinking," people would say. I believe, my dear Lucy, this was about the time you quit watering our wine. Mel used to say that you were taking nips and then adding water to make up the difference. "What do I care?" I answered. "Let her drink the whole bottle." But you did come home from your days off a bit tipsy.

Then you stopped. Was it because of your new church? You said they wanted everyone to "speak right out."

"All at once?" I asked.

"When the words come," you said.

Did you "speak in tongues," Lucy?

You were married in that church, Lucy. In a new dress and new shoes. (Which I did not approve of. "Lucy, you need your money to build a house on your property," I yelled. Why didn't I buy the dress and shoes?)

Did I do you good in the long run, Lucy, with my

DO THIS
DON'T DO THAT . . .

You needed a religion that would fit your time and place, Lucy. One that would marry you. One that didn't ask for money to decorate an altar with gold.

You used to tell me how the church people came to your little home in the country when you were a child. They came to ask for money. You said, "My mother had a toothache; my father was away; I was home from school because there was no school. The young man who was our teacher drank. He also bothered the girls."

"You didn't tell this to the padres?"

"We were afraid."

I hope you were buried properly by your new church, Lucy. And by your husband. He inherited your property, Lucy. "I have a son," he said to me when I was in Chile on my visit. "Just one child. I married an older woman a year after Lucy died."

It's OK, Lucy. Your land will go on.

I'm Waiting for
My Brain to Evolve

"God only knows."
We say that every day,
as casually as applesauce.
Actually
it says it all.
GOD ONLY KNOWS.
Our brains
have not evolved
further than that.

Wonder, Nature & Rituals

I hear science talking
but I see the mountains breathe.
Part of me would like to be a revolutionary.
Part of me would like to sing and dance
in the garden of the Lord.
Part of me would like to be a glacier lily.

10 Spring Rituals

"Is that a dandelion salad?" Mel asked. "I'm not sure I'm crazy about dandelion salad."

"Would you rather have sulfur and molasses?" I asked. I've never had sulfur and molasses in my whole life. I don't know anyone who has, but everyone talks about it so it must have been a custom at one time. It was a spring tonic. Maybe it was more. Maybe it was a ritual—as if spring couldn't come unless everyone swallowed that spoonful of sulfur and molasses.

Psychologists say we need rituals. We don't have the same ones our ancestors had, so maybe we have to make our own.

I have very definite rituals of spring. (And summer, and fall, and winter.) I have to do them, one by one, carefully and thoroughly, or the world couldn't progress in its journey out of one month into the next. At least I couldn't progress. Like the giant Antaeus, who had to touch his feet to Earth to hold on to his strength, I have to live in the seasons. Right here and now I have to dig the first new dandelions of spring and make a salad and eat it with awe and reverence. Spring Has Come!

You don't need the same set of rituals I have. Perhaps it's one of the secrets of life you have to discover on your own:

My 10 Spring Rituals

1) Actually make a dandelion salad. In large cities you can buy the greens in the market. For example, people grow dandelions on farms in New Jersey. In the suburbs, people grow them on their lawns.

2) Make a Checklist for Spring and tape it to the refrigerator door. (See my list on page 185. This list is to help spring come.)

3) Buy a notebook and write on the cover *Nature Journal*. This is not a bare list. It's for thoughts, observations and comparisons of one year to another. This is where you write, *Hello, glacier lily, you are early this year. Last year you didn't open your yellow blossoms until April 3rd.* Also, this is where you write questions to yourself: *Is it possible the number of crows in the city is increasing? Why?* Nature is a friend. You have to meet it, greet it, bless it and pay homage.

I include both wildflowers and garden flowers in my notebook. Why not? The first time I see a red tulip in someone's garden it makes my heart jump the same as a wild trillium. A group of six daffodils under a birch tree in a backyard is a very satisfactory sight. Remember that poem by Wordsworth?

> *A host of golden daffodils*
> *beside the lake,*
> *beside the trees,*
> *dancing and fluttering in the breeze . . .*

Once I saw that poem in real life. We were in Canada above Glacier Park. We rounded a turn and there was a lake and a hillside—with a host of daffodils dancing and fluttering in the breeze. They were wild on that hillside. I ran from the car and trespassed on someone's property. I didn't pick the daffodils, but I sort of hugged them.

City flowers aren't like that, but in a way they're more important because we need them so much.

4) Plan a day to Search for Spring. I do it every year. A cattail swamp is the best place. Spring comes early around swamps. You'll be walking in ice and snow and slush, but you might hear the honk honk of Canadian geese flying north. You can listen for the rusty voice of the redwinged blackbird. When you spot the bird, say to him (go ahead, you can speak to birds—there's no law against it)—say, "You sound a bit rusty, my friend. You'll have to practice before you sing to your lady friend."

Maybe the new shoots of the cattail will be out. You can gather enough to add to your lunchtime salad.

5) Identify one new flower or bird. Last year I walked 10 miles for a steershead. It's a flower, so tiny you have to kneel to see any detail, but it looks exactly like the skull of a steer. It's not showy, and it grows out on a bare, gravelly mountainside. It blooms just as the snowpack recedes so you have to hike up a trail that goes, in spots, through deep snowdrifts.

So why am I clucking like a mother hen who just found a worm? I think it's like the birdwatchers who put a notch on their walking-stick when they finally see a great horned owl. I've looked at the picture of steershead in my wildflower book for 12 years. Now I have gone, I have seen, I have conquered.

But I did not pick. I did not dig.

If there isn't a group of wildflower enthusiasts in your area, try a birdwatching group. Look in your paper to see if there is a Saturday hike and go along. You might want to ask how strenuous the hike will be. I'm thinking of the Audubon Society field trip I went on. Before it was half over, I felt as if I'd fallen into a marathon.

"Is it possible," I said to myself, "that these people are trying to get rid of me?" They climbed up to Mission Falls and the trail was so steep—well, there was no trail at all. There was just a mountain-goat slide. How can you climb up a slide? I was so scared that I couldn't eat my lunch. I knew I had to come back down, and I could see myself sliding down three counties and landing in Wyoming.

But I did see a rare bird (I forget the name) and some lovely Indian pipe, which is not too common in our area.

6) Invite friends over for a Spring Fling lunch of lamb's-quarter omelet and rhubarb pie.

I know rhubarb pie might overload your system with sugar, and how about the fat in the crust (even if the flour is whole-wheat), and how about the oxalate salts in both the lamb's quarter and the rhubarb? You're right. Sometimes I fling caution to the winds and say "FULL SPEED AHEAD!" I must celebrate spring, and for me spring means lamb's-quarter omelet and rhubarb pie.

And a bouquet of lilacs on the table too. That's my May ritual—my alley ritual. In Missoula in May you meet the best people in the alley, walking, smelling, sniffing. You have to do that in May. Bury your nose in every lilac bush up and down the street, or alley. Cut some lilacs (from your own bush—don't "borrow" them), put them on your lunch table, eat your lunch and bless spring and all it stands for. IT CAME, DIDN'T IT?

While you're digesting the lunch, take down your book of poetry and read *When Lilacs Last In the Dooryard Bloom'd*. That's a spring ritual too.

7) Go on a morel-mushroom hunt, even if you don't intend to find any. I never do. My students pick them all before I get there. I think I've taught too many classes. Now I have to buy my mushrooms in the store, but I don't mind. The walk, the hike, the search is the thing.

8) Plant something—in the ground. A garden—organic of course—or a field of potatoes. Or a bunch of chives in a pot for your window sill. Put your fingers in the earth—Mother Earth, your mother, your earth.

9) Walk on a yellow carpet of fallen maple blossoms. There's about one week when you can do that. Some people will walk their mother to church on Mother's Day on a yellow carpet. Some years it all comes together.

10) Whistle back at the evening grosbeaks in the elm trees—if there are any elm trees left in your neighborhood. Otherwise, holler at a robin while he's pulling a worm out of your lawn. Lean out of the window and say, "Hi, sport."

Checklist for Spring

You know how they say faith can move mountains? This checklist, if kept faithfully by each and every one of us, will Bring Spring—I promise you.

You can copy this chart from the book and paste it in your nature notebook or pin it on your bulletin board or tape it to the refrigerator.

EVENT	DATE	PLACE
Snowdrop in bloom		
Crocus in bloom		
Pussy willow in bloom		
V of Canada geese going north		
Skunk cabbage poking through marsh		
Rhubarb crowns showing in garden		
Violet in bloom		
First robin on lawn		
First daffodil open		
Heard song of meadowlark		
Buttercup in bloom		
Trillium in bloom		
Dogtooth violet in bloom		
Saw a kite flying		
Raked lawn		
Got a sunburn		
Sound of lawnmower		
Put away snow shovel		
Brought out hose		
Smiled at neighbor and said, "Spring is here."		

You fill in your own dates and locations. You can add more events to the list or make a completely new one.

The Bluebird of Happiness

I was sitting there waiting for a bluebird. The bluebird of happiness? I didn't think so, but wait a minute. How often in life does one have time to sit on the ground by a telephone pole waiting for a bluebird to come back to its nest?

The nest was in a birdhouse attached to the telephone pole in the yard of our friends, the Ottens, up on Echo Lake.

The reason I was watching the nest was this: There was a duel going on between the male bluebird and some swallows. The female bluebird was inside the house. No doubt she had eggs there. This was mating season; it would be logical she had eggs in a nest and was sitting on them.

According to Jane Otten, the birdhouse was regulation size, styled by the Audubon Society.

But the swallows didn't seem to be convinced of that. The previous year a pair had nested in the bluebird house. "It was terrible," Jane said. "The bluebirds were here—a pair of them—and they wanted to nest in the house, but the swallows got there first."

This year the bluebirds arrived first. "Is it the same pair that tried last year?" I asked.

"I don't know," Jane said. "It would be nice to think so."

"It has to be a tough bluebird," I said, "because evidently he has to defend his territory. Here come the swallows."

Two swallows swooped down and flew right over the birdhouse. Swish! The male bluebird immediately flew at them. The swallows retreated. I was a little surprised. The bluebird was only a tiny bit larger than the swallows, and there were two of them.

"That's a feisty bluebird," I said to Jane. "How long will he have to guard his domain?"

"Probably until the eggs hatch," Jane said. "The swallows usually nest in the garage, but evidently they have their eye on this bird-house." The male bluebird had his watchpost on the near corner of the garage.

"He doesn't seem to mind us," I said.

"No," Jane said, "he likes people. Sometimes when I'm leading the horses to the barn, he'll swoop down and fly right along beside me. He almost touches my shoulder."

"That's the bluebird of happiness," I said.

KIM WILLIAMS'

A Good Laugh on April Fool's Day Is Worth $10

Is it silly to fool someone on April Fool's day—to put strings in the pancakes (Mel's mother did that every year) or "plant" full-grown radishes by the light of the moon? How can we spend time "fooling" when the world is in a state of *chassis?* (I love that word. It comes from Sean O'Casey's play *Juno and the Paycock.* The character using it meant *chaos.*)

Sean O'Casey wrote that play in the 1920s. But we can go back to the Middle Ages (read Barbara Tuchman's book on the 14th century, *A Distant Mirror)* or the Stone Age—any time. Maybe the world has always been in a state of *chassis.* In between, we have little spaces of peace and quiet—halcyon days. During these halcyon days (Were the '50s our halcyon days?) we start thinking this is the norm.

I'll be serious April 2. I'll get mad about two or three things, holler at one or two people, maybe write a letter to the editor.

But April 1 is fool's day. Remember how the kings of old had a fool—a jester? Things certainly weren't rosy in those days. Everyone had a toothache. You got pneumonia every time you took a bath. When you became sick, you either got better or you died.

If we can judge from Shakespeare, it wasn't only kings who had a fool. The ordinary people "jested" also.

When we lived in South America and mixed with those European-oriented people, we continually were amazed by the amount of jesting that went on, among the rich and the poor.

I think the Latins were continually amazed how serious we Americans were. "You have so much more than we do, yet you worry so much," they'd say to us. Maybe one hinges on the other?

Some jokes that South Americans played on each other were very elaborate. One I remember concerned a dinner of fish ducks. This was cooked up (literally) by our Spanish friend Jorge. These fish ducks that the hunters were hunting were not edible—almost everyone knew that. But Jorge invited all the hunters who had been on a certain expedition to a fish-duck dinner that he would personally prepare.

Of course Jorge cooked ordinary barnyard ducks. "Delicious," everyone said, and they rushed home with their fish ducks, cleaned them oh so carefully, and followed the same recipe that Jorge had used to cook his "fish ducks." Well, you can imagine the results. Jorge had to hide for three days.

I don't think we should indulge in that kind of a joke. I simply believe a gentle little nudge toward laughter might be welcome April 1.

Mel says that even though he and his brother and his sister knew there would be strings in the pancakes on April Fool's day (after all, it happened every year), nevertheless, the whole family joined in the joke, laughing and kidding each other.

A good laugh is worth $10. It's worth as much as eating out. I expect Mel to fool me on April Fool's day. He always does.

You do the same. Fool someone. Or maybe it's your turn to be fooled. Don't get mad if someone plays a joke on you. Laugh and say "Thank you."

A Mountain Spring
Is a Marvelous Thing

I knew it was a privilege to sit near this mountain spring bubbling out of the ground like the fountain of youth. Mel and I had back-packed to a mountain lake, and while he fished I sat in an alpine meadow and observed the spring.

I had to put my hand in the welling-out of water to see what the magic force was. There *was* a force to the water—it actually pushed on my hand.

I sat as close to the spring as I could without falling in. I almost didn't know how to relate to this event. In the modern world water comes out of a faucet. Remotely we know it comes out of a reservoir somewhere, and it's chlorinated and maybe filtered.

But a spring is something as fundamental as creation. It is water bubbling out of the ground. It has a slow rhythm like a heartbeat. You can feel the pulse.

I sat so still a dragonfly landed on my head. I felt it and then I saw it fly away—a blue dragonfly, not at all worried. It probably thought I was a tree or a post.

A yellow bee flew by and hesitated as if it were about to argue with me. Over the spring? Over a clump of beargrass? A group of shootingstars?

I was sitting in a bower of wildflowers, an alpine meadow filled with bog orchids, elephanthead, white violets, cowslips. In alpine meadows in midsummer you find spring flowers—you actually go back to spring. There were wild strawberries in bloom. Would they ever produce fruit?

There had been mosquitoes in the early morning, but now it was almost noon and they had gone. "Mel and I will have lunch in this grassy paradise," I said. "We'll watch the spring like Old Faithful."

I started cleaning out the spring so we could fill our canteens. By the time Mel arrived the water was running clear and clean again.

"There should be a frog," I said to Mel. "We always had a frog in our spring on the farm. He jumped out when you cleaned the spring."

Mel had grown up on a farm too, so he knew about springs and cleaning them by dipping out all the water, pail by pail. You had to dip faster than the water came in.

A frog always jumped out while you were cleaning the spring. Only one. I don't remember ever seeing more than one frog in a spring. I wonder why. Is it like robins in a garden? You might at times have more than one, but one seems to be resident.

After cleaning out the spring on our farm, I always sat there watching it fill. It was, after all, the miraculous pitcher. No matter how much water you took out of the spring it was still full.

And the frog came back. Odd that we never questioned the right of that frog to be in our drinking water.

Mel went back to his fishing, and I stayed at the spring. Was I waiting for the resident frog? Would there be frogs at this high-mountain spring? Maybe the dragonfly was the resident spirit.

My husband and I would not be residents. We had backpacked in, and we would backpack out. A spring like this and a lake like this don't need any other permanent residents than a dragonfly, a deer, a bee, and maybe some small trout.

Walking Alone in Lolo National Forest

I was walking in Lolo National Forest. By myself. Well, not really. I was with Mel. But I told him to go on ahead. He wanted to explore the top of the ridge. I was content with the middle of the ridge.

I didn't mind being left behind. Actually I enjoyed it. There's a different feeling entirely when you're by yourself on a mountain trail. You sort of hear the forest, but you hear it in a way you never do when you're with people. At least I don't. Because I'm talking. Oh, I'm a talker. But when I'm by myself it's a different world. Have you tried it?

Now, don't overdo it. People shouldn't be alone in mountains. Suppose an emergency came along. But for an hour or so it's as if you were in the Garden of Eden and everything about you is new and green. The birds make small calls. You hear the wind soughing in the pines. I hope the wind is soughing; maybe it's *sue-ing,* or *sowing.* Anyway, it's a sound that goes with green forests and mountains and wide blue skies.

I sat down to listen. By a creek. It was rippling down the mountainside. I took out my tin cup and drank a cup of water. So pure and clean. Who was talking about bottled Perrier water the other day? It's from a spring, and the French bottle the water and sell it all over the world.

"Maybe some day Montana will bottle this water right here," I said to myself. Pure and clean, it'll go to New York and Louisiana and Los Angeles. Just for drinking, not for flushing toilets and washing cars. I don't doubt at all that some day we'll have two water systems: one for drinking and one for flushing toilets and so on. Actually we may not flush toilets at all in the future. We'll make mulch for the soil instead.

These are the kinds of thoughts that go through your mind when you're sitting near a mountain creek in a national forest.

I closed my eyes to listen better to the forest. It's true, you do hear better when you close your eyes. I heard a raven. He was croaking, but it was a very short croak, sort of a "Well?" and then a "Hey." He was just being friendly.

I would no doubt have heard more, but my husband came back from his exploring. The first thing he said was, "You'd better check for ticks."

I jumped up. I'd forgotten all about ticks. Sure enough, I had one on my pant leg and one on my sock. A person has to be very careful hiking in the Rockies because the ticks can carry Rocky Mountain spotted tick fever. "I was thinking about water," I said.

"With your eyes shut? If you had fallen asleep, you'd have tumbled down the mountain like this rock." Mel loosened a rock, rolled it over the edge of the trail. It bumpety-bumped down the mountain. It took a long time to get to the bottom.

I suppose we should take a lesson here. When you're out hiking, don't sit down in tick country and don't close your eyes on a mountain trail.

But do listen to the wind in the trees and do look at the water rippling down the mountainside. And do think about it.

Ladybirds on Top
of Squaw Peak

Could these be ladybirds? What would those sweet little ladybird bugs be doing on top of a bare mountain peak?

But there they were—above timberline on a bare rock slide.

Mel and I were on top of Squaw Peak. The day was cool and breezy but not windy. You can tell that the top of Squaw Peak is usually windy. Even before you reach the rockpile top the few remaining pine trees are so small and misshapen you know the wind is blowing a gale here most of the time. The few branches that are on the scrubby trees are all on one side, as if the storms just blew the branches right off. I don't know how these trees have the courage to even try living on this barren mountain.

So what possessed these little ladybird bugs to be on top of Squaw Peak? Were they lost? Were they out of their minds? No. They had a purpose. I know because other people have seen them on other mountain tops. My friend Will said he was on top of McLeod Peak once and it was so cold and snowy and windy he could hardly stay a minute, and yet the ladybird bugs were there.

You know what a ladybird bug looks like. It's that tiny orange and black spotted beetle—a flying beetle—that children sing about: "Ladybird, ladybird, fly away home. Your house is on fire and your children are gone."

Nobody harms the ladybirds because we all know they are beneficial. People pay money to buy packages of them to let loose in their gardens. Ladybirds, or ladybugs—you can call them by either name—eat aphids. Somewhere I heard they eat 50 or 60 aphids per day.

But how would you feel if you spent $10 buying ladybirds and then you climbed a mountain and all your ladybirds were on top of the mountain?

In masses. A Forest Service man told me you can find 50 pounds of ladybirds in one spot. 50 pounds! "But don't go and put those 50 pounds in a pail and bring them down from the mountain," he said. I know those ladybugs are going through a cycle. They need to be on top of the mountain. They'll come down in their own good time and they'll each eat 50 aphids a day. But then they have to go back up the mountain.

Can you imagine a tiny little ladybug flying from a garden down in the valley all the way to the top of a mountain peak 8000 feet up?

And it's not even safe. Bears lift up the rocks and scoop the ladybugs into their mouths by the shovelful.

> Ladybird, ladybird, don't fly away.
> Spend the winter under the eaves
> of my garage.

How foolish I am. Nature does what it does and it doesn't matter if we understand or not.

I Hope I Survive This Trip

First it was the deer knocking the tent over. Can you imagine complaining about such a thing? I mean, you go into the wilderness to see deer and there I was, shooing them away.

Well, I couldn't sleep. Snuffle, snuffle around the tent. "Is that a bear?" I asked Mel.

"That's a deer snorting," he said.

"Why would a deer snort?" I asked.

"I don't know," Mel said. "Go to sleep."

But how could I go to sleep with all that snorting around—bumping over the tent ropes, chewing grass right under the front flap of the tent?

Now, I know this doesn't happen everywhere, but the Meadow Lake area in the Scapegoat Wilderness seems to have a special kind of deer. That afternoon I was sitting by a little stream when I looked up and there was a deer, a sweet doe, nonchalantly cropping grass 20 feet from me.

But in the middle of the night! I know deer feed at dusk and of course you go to bed at dusk when you camp out. You're not going to pack a lantern in your backpack. After sundown you go to bed.

And then comes this snort snort, shuffle shuffle, crop crop. "Why right here?" I said to Mel. "Why right around our tent? There's plenty of grass everywhere."

"Go to sleep," Mel said.

Snort snort, shuffle shuffle, crackle crackle. Well, I finally dozed off. Then I was really bounced out of bed—literally! The ground shook like an earthquake. It was a thunderbolt. Then came more. Thunder and lightning. Crash bang! "What'll we do?" I asked.

There was no point in Mel's answering me. When you're backpacking and you're in your sleeping bag in your pup tent, what can you do? Are you going to go running off into the downpour?

There's nothing to do but be calm about the whole thing. Thunder and lightning are so big and you're so small out there in the wilderness, what can you say? "I hope I survive. If not, it's been a good trip."

But I tell you I was mighty happy when it calmed down. The rain poured for hours, but that was a lullaby compared to the thunder and lightning.

The next day, of course, our clothes and boots were wet through in a minute. Well, you can't expect perfection on a camping trip—not a whole trip. You can expect only moments here and there. Just like in ordinary life—little moments here and there.

10 Ways To Hold On to Summer

I made a list of ways to hold on to summer. You have to hold on to summer with both hands because it goes so fast. I have 10 things on my list, and I have to do them at least once. Some I do every day, if I can.

1) Burying my nose in roses is something I do every single day. I walk wherever I have to go, and I bury my nose in rosebushes up and down the street. No doubt by now everyone in Missoula thinks I'm a little odd: "There goes Mrs. Williams. She doesn't drive. She walks up and down the streets in rain and in shine. When the lilacs were in bloom, she walked up and down the streets burying her nose in every lilac bush there was. Now the roses are in bloom and here she is. She is likely to say, 'Good morning, may I bury my nose in your rose?' "

It's true—I do that. When the crabapples were in bloom I was walking, and I came to a tree that was a giant mass of pink. Every inch of the tree was covered with huge blooms. I said to the gentleman in the garden, "Your crabapple tree is like a fluffy bear. I want to hug it." Of course he thought I was crazy, but he smiled and said, "It's never been so full of bloom."

"I bet you take very good care of it," I said and then I walked on.

I inherited this trait from my father. He talked to everybody. "Good morning, madam," he would say to complete strangers. We were embarrassed. Now I'm doing the same. May I bury my nose in your rose?

But we can take a little time off, can't we? This is June. If we don't stop in June to hold on to roses and violets and lilies, the 10th day of June will turn into the 15th and then the 20th and first thing you know it'll be the 25th and then the 30th and June will be gone and did we stop to say "Your roses are so beautiful," to a neighbor? Did we cut a bouquet for Mrs. Jones? Did we put three perfect petals in the gelatin salad for the church supper?

The world won't go to pot if we stop a minute in June.

2) I have to picnic in a ferny dell where fairies dwell. Maybe that spot exists only in my dreams. Maybe I'll have to settle for a reservoir where ducks quack, but that's OK.

3) I want to walk in a field of daisies, calm and still. Spring Gulch in the Rattlesnake Canyon is such a spot. It's filled with ox-eye daisies, those plain, ordinary field daisies that make you think of cows chewing their cud and children saying, "He loves me, he loves me not."

Once a year I walk in this field of daisies, and I sing to myself. It's a song I made up—a little nothing, but it's the essence of summer to me. It goes like this:

> *Field of daisies,*
> *calm and still—*
> *sunny sunny summer.*
> *Smile a while, bide a while—*
> *sunny sunny summer.*

Corny, of course. But tell me, doesn't a field of daisies seem to you like all the innocence left in the world? Shy little maidens all in white, standing in an open meadow.

I'll probably find a handful of ripe strawberries in among the daisies. I'll eat them. They are nectar and ambrosia.

4) I shall climb a mountain. Sit on the top like a buddha, and think. At least, I'll meditate a little.

5) I shall pick raspberries on Bastille Day. That's the day the French Revolution started, or was it won on that day? Anyway, Bastille Day is the 14th of July, and our raspberries are ripe just about then.

Maybe this is the way the world has always been. In between

revolutions and earthquakes—uprisings and churnings—people pick raspberries.

6) I'm going to sit in my own backyard, under my own maple tree, on a summer evening. Just sit quietly and say to myself, "Oh, these lovely summer evenings that last forever."

7) I'm going to smell summer—that deep, hot, hazy smell of summer. I'm going to breathe it in—yes, in town—yes, along a river—yes, on a mountain ridge—the deep, sweet smell of summer.

8) I want to walk in a hayfield, a newly mown hayfield. I don't know why, but I get a pang in my heart when I ride past a meadow of newly mown hay. Is it the hay that is cut that once was grass? No, that can't be it. Is it my childhood when I walked in stubblefields and turned the hay with a fork? And then when the hay was in the barn, jumped in it with glory and, oh yes, trepidation. It was a little scary to jump from the rafters.

A hayfield always has the slow drone of bees and the hot midday sun coming straight down—so you don't leave a shadow—and chokecherry bushes growing along the creek.

9) I'll go to a rummage sale and buy some extra canning jars. Make ready for harvest time. Make ready for winter.

10) At the end of summer I'll get into a cause. You can call it a project. Windpower, or local government, or save the farms from a dust bowl. I'll have the energy then, the strength that I got from the mountains, the rivers, the field of daisies, the roses.

That's what summer is for—so we can be ready for fall—the work that needs to be done.

A Golden Huckleberry Day Baked into a Pie

Is it possible to be sitting in a huckleberry patch at 12 noon and be eating the pie at five in the afternoon? We did that.

Even though the weather forecast said rain, we went anyway. You have to do that. Take some plastic garbage sacks along for raingear, wear shoes that have non-skid soles, and go. Sometimes the weather surprises you. Then you have an unexpected beautiful day. Even half a day. Even an hour in between showers. If you stay home waiting for a perfect day, maybe the berries will come and go and you'll still be waiting.

The sun came out and there we were on top of the mountain with a green valley below, green forests across the valley, white clouds overhead and a blue sky—so clean and so blue.

It doesn't really matter if you find berries or not when you're on top of a mountain and it's so quiet all you hear are small sounds of birds, and even they are far away.

You go up a mountain for more than berries. I have a friend—she's retired and could live anywhere—who said to me, "It's because of the huckleberries I live in Montana." She didn't mean just the fruit—the berries that are really blueberries and not huckleberries.

(I have to mention that right here or I'll get a few letters correcting me, one from my Forest Service friend here in Missoula who objects whenever I use the word *huckleberry* in a newspaper article.

He calls me up. "You've done it again," he says sternly.

"I know," I say. "I know these berries are really blueberries, speaking scientifically, but people love to call them huckleberries and you know yourself they taste more like New England huckleberries than they do blueberries.")

Whatever people want to call these berries doesn't matter. The point is you don't go up a mountain just for berries, and my friend Allison doesn't live in Montana just to pick huckleberries.

Picking wild berries is—well, it's a kind of connection. Maybe to a hill you walked on when you were 10. Maybe your neighbor invited you along on a picnic and there were berries on the hill and the sun was shining and you remember a blue pail and you remember a woodchuck and a small creek where you ate the picnic lunch.

The rocks were warm where you sat to eat your lunch. How many things you have forgotten since you were 10, and yet you remember the blue pail and the rocks that were warm from the sun.

We didn't pick a lot of berries on our expedition. There were three of us, and all we got was enough for two pies. People had already picked in this patch. It was late in the season. The berries we did get were beginning to wrinkle.

None of that mattered because we had a day we didn't expect. It was supposed to rain, but we started out anyway. We climbed the mountain. Then the sun came out. We found some berries. We put the berries in the pail along with the sun and the mountain and the forest and the faraway sounds of the birds.

We brought all that down the mountain and baked it into a pie. A golden day baked into a huckleberry pie with a golden crust.

Lucy, my Lucy in South America, used to say to me, "We must celebrate the earth." Picking wild berries is doing that.

And Kim Will Bring
a Jug of Water

"And Kim Williams will bring a jug of water." That sounds terrible. It was part of a potluck picnic and I'll never live it down. It sounds as if I'm going to a potluck picnic and all I'm bringing is a jug of water. What I meant was that in addition to the other things I was going to bring—I would bring a jug of water.

Well, you know how you can go on a picnic and it's like "Water, water everywhere and not a drop to drink." There's Coca-Cola, lemon soda, orange pop, Dr. Pepper, Mountain Dew, two kinds of beer, maybe even wine—but there's no water. When you're really thirsty, there is nothing that will quench your thirst but plain water—not even lemonade or apple juice. You want plain water.

I wouldn't think of going on a picnic without a jug of water. I don't drink any of that other stuff. Well, I drink a little wine sometimes, but not on a picnic. Oh, I know, a picnic—if it's a deluxe picnic, European-style—is cheese and wine, a loaf of French bread and some fruit. A plain, true-blue American picnic is fried chicken, potato salad, chocolate cake and ice cream.

Whatever kind of picnic you choose, don't work too hard. I think many times we work too hard on a picnic—cooking for hours and then you need an icebox and you have to eat at a certain time and what do you do with the leftovers?

Our hiking club has learned a lot from the backpackers. Keep it simple. Take food that time will not demolish. Good bread, cheese, nuts, fruit, raw vegetables. A canteen of water.

Then you have time to walk along the river. Somebody is always there to identify the trees. Somebody knows the birds. We look for mushrooms. We admire the flowers.

Sometimes when you feast your stomach too much you don't have any strength left to feast your eyes and your ears and your nose.

Summer is a feast for all your senses. The clouds and the sky and the green everywhere is a feast for the eyes. The songs of the birds, the sound of the wind in the trees, the sound of a river or a stream— that's a feast for the ears. And the nose—well, the nose has flowers and berries and the fruit that is ripe on the trees, and the morning at dawn and the evening after the sun is gone but the smell of leaves and shrubs is still aromatic from the heat of the day.

A picnic is a time for all that. So keep it simple. And do bring a jug of water, even if you get a reputation.

Knee-deep in Cherries and Raspberries

I'm standing in my kitchen and I'm knee-deep in cherries, and up to my elbows in raspberries. Steam from the canning kettle is rising to the ceiling. My fingers are blue. The fingernails are worn down to the nub. I'm barefoot.

No, I'm not pressing the juice out of the cherries and raspberries with my bare feet. It's hot here, and I'm working very hard. It's that time of year. Time to put away for winter the bounty of summer. Get up early, go to bed late. Last night I was boiling cherries at midnight.

I'm not suffering. I love it all. It's not just the idea of having home-canned fruit in winter, although that's marvelous. That's only part of it. The rest is the whole process of watching the trees and shrubs blossom in spring, then turn into fruit that is small and green at first, and then gets bigger and fatter and finally bursts into ripeness.

And then falls into my hand. My hands practice opening and closing for a whole month ahead of the gathering season. That's true. One day I was walking home from downtown and all of a sudden I noticed I was talking to myself and my right hand was opening and closing. It's a good thing I didn't meet anyone I knew.

In my mind's eye I was in the cherry orchards on Flathead Lake and my hands all by themselves were reaching up to pluck and gather and pick those big, fat, glossy cherries.

If we visit the orchards ahead of picking time, I have to hold on to my right hand with my left hand to keep it from illegally reaching up to those branches. The gathering instinct is that strong in me.

Oh, I know we have fruit all year round in the stores. I'm glad we do. But it's not the same as picking your own. Maybe it's the ritual of the trees, the smell of the leaves, the sun and the air in the orchard.

And the fruit is so ripe. Stores can't handle really ripe fruit. It doesn't keep, and they lose money. But when you pick your own you can wait. Oh, I love ripe fruit, warm from the sun. Some people don't. They like it ice-cold from the refrigerator—strawberries on shaved ice, nectarines so icy-cold that dew forms on them when you take them out of the cooler.

I also know very ripe fruit doesn't make the best jam—with the best consistency, I mean. But I don't care about that. I don't make perfect jam anyway. Mine is a sort of fruit preserve. I use very little sugar because the fruit is so ripe. I just boil it up and put it into sterilized jars and seal it.

I boil the cherries in their own juice. I don't make a canning syrup at all.

I also freeze fruit. That's less work, and it preserves more of the flavor and the vitamins. But the feeling isn't the same. There's something about this time of the year that calls for being knee-deep in cherries and raspberries and canning kettles and steam rising to the ceiling.

Coming to Terms with Fall

There is a day when you know the year has slipped over the crest of summer. For each person the knowledge comes in a different way. With me, it's my nose that tells me. I squeeze my eyes shut and say, "No, no, never!" but my nose sniffs the air and says, "It's different."

There is a definite end-of-summer smell. It's not just one thing—it's made up of many things: drying grass, hot pine forests (too hot—there will be forest fires if we drop a match), dust in the air, pollen, flowers turning into fruit, seeds dropping to the ground.

The end-of-summer flowers have a different smell from the early-summer flowers. Of course it may be my imagination, but asters and goldenrod seem to me to have a poignant smell. Hold on to every day, they say, summer is at its height. Fall is just a breath away.

Every year I avoid speaking the word *aster*, and the word *goldenrod*, as long as I can. I know I have to come to terms with fall—we have to do that every year—but I turn my head: "Not yet," I say. "Not yet."

But my nose tells me. I'll be walking on a high ridge and the smell of giant hyssop comes wafting on the air. Hyssop is a mint. All the mints have a powerful smell in late summer.

Berries will be falling off the bushes or drying up on the bushes. I'll smell huckleberry, elderberry, black raspberry.

Do leaves turning red and yellow have a different smell? Yes, they do. Dogbane is already yellow; hawthorn is already red.

I can smell apples. I can smell pears. Like an old hound dog I'm sniffing and smelling, and the message that goes to my brain is this: You have a little time left—go. Go at a moment's notice. If someone calls you to go berrying, go. Don't let time, weather or work stop you. One last trip to look at flowers. One last trip to pick herbs to dry.

Get up early, go to bed late. Don't tie yourself to dinner at 6 and TV news at 7. Eat a simple repast and go. You can dine in winter.

The night sky is beautiful. Remember when you came home at 2 a.m. and you had to stop the car to look and then look again? Remember those silver clouds, that white moon, the blue-black sky?

Instead of hollering, "Where did the summer go?"—you go. You can sleep in winter, like the bears do.

All this my nose tells me. And I'm listening.

The Destiny of Canning Jars

I knew it would happen. When my husband brought home a dozen canning jars from the Senior Citizens rummage sale—"A present," he said. "I paid only 10 cents apiece"—I said, "Oh, that's fine. Thank you very much," but I didn't jump up and down.

We'd already filled all the jars we had—with apricots, cherries, raspberries, serviceberries, elderberries. I was ready to say *amen*, finis for this harvest season.

"Put the jars away for next summer," Mel said.

I knew it wasn't that easy. Empty jars aren't happy. They want to sit fat and full on the pantry shelf. That is their destiny and destiny must be fulfilled.

I'll test that theory, I said. I'll put these jars in the basement, out of sight. And when I walk around town, I won't even look at an apple tree or a pear tree or anything to do with produce.

Comes Labor Day and a person is different. You've been away for the summer—maybe not physically but your mind is away—gone fishing. But after Labor Day you're back. You've joined the human race. You read the editorial page of the newspaper. You call up the mayor. In a small town you can do that. Well, you can do it in a big city too, but it's easier in a small town.

You go to a City Council meeting; you volunteer for the school board. Maybe you go to school. Sign up for an art course. Go to a lecture, give a lecture, carry a petition—all that belongs to fall.

The year really begins in fall—not in January. I think it has something to do with the blood. The blood courses through your veins. Well, it always does that, but you can depend upon it in the fall. There's an extra vitality you might not have later on. So if you are going to do a project, now is the time.

That's why I said to myself, "I'm going to make believe these empty jars don't exist. I'm into other things now. My blood is coursing through my veins. My mind is ready to percolate. I have to study, learn, teach, go to meetings, move the universe one millionth of one centimeter forward." (I'm being funny. Does anyone move the universe even one millionth of one centimeter either forward or backward?)

My small point is that if you're going to do anything, fall is the time to do it. So OUT with those canning jars—to the cellar, the basement, the garage. That's what I said.

Guess what is sitting on the kitchen floor. A box of apples. I know why. Those jars sent out tentacles like an octopus. They attracted the apples.

They're lovely apples, but not the kind you can store.

I could give them away. After all, somebody gave them to me. No, it's no use. These jars will simply attract something else. They'll keep sending out their tentacles. So I'll make the applesauce. The universe will have to wait.

A Pantry Is Like a Fall Painting

I was in my neighbor's pantry. A pantry is a marvelous sight—if it's the kind of pantry that has jars of home-canned peaches and pears and jam and jelly and pickles.

That's the kind my neighbor has. "This is like a painting," I said. "You could just take a brush and lots of red and yellow and gold and you could paint all these jars and call the picture *Autumn* or maybe *Autumn Harvest.*"

"Oh, I don't paint," my neighbor said.

Well, she doesn't have to. She's painting pictures right there in that pantry. I had to sit down on the floor and just admire. All the jars were in rows, and the colors were all the fall shades.

The peaches were bright yellow; the pears were pale gold; the plums were deep pink, almost purple.

I saw she had buffaloberry jelly. Not many people know buffaloberry jelly. The berry grows only in the West, but the oldtime Indians and early white settlers used it a great deal, as a sauce with buffalo meat.

That's where the name came from—*buffaloberry* because it was eaten along with buffalo meat. The berry grows on scrubby-looking bushes, rather dry-looking, not at all handsome. The berry is small and red, rather like a currant, but it does not hang in bunches as currants do. Buffaloberries grow right on the branches of the bush.

And there are thorns. You can get scratched trying to pick the berries. And they aren't especially tasty either. They're sour and even a little bitter. You can see that the Indians and early settlers used fruit that you and I would probably leave right on the bushes.

But buffaloberry jelly is quite good. It has a tang and just the right amount of tartness. The color is perfect amber. If you were painting that color, you'd use a blush pink with a touch of peach in it.

Anyway, my neighbor had six little jars of this lovely jelly on her shelf. Next to those she had currant jelly, sparkling red, then crabapple jelly with a color halfway between the red of the currant and the amber of the buffaloberry.

On the shelf below the jellies were watermelon pickles—not the dyed-green kind. No, these were a natural honey color. Then came canned cherries—dark red, almost black. Then apricots. Oh, what a color home-canned apricots have—if you find apricots when they are just right—sweet as nectar and red-orange in color.

"What would we do without glass jars?" I said to my neighbor. "Fruit in tin cans doesn't do anything for the soul."

My neighbor laughed. "I rarely buy anything in stores," she said. "I can so much."

"Do you put the jars on the shelves in a special order or just as you work on them?" I asked. All the different colors seemed to fit together so perfectly. A painter would spend hours arranging and rearranging this material.

"I think it just happened," my neighbor said. "But I will put my applesauce right here next to the apricots. I don't know why. Maybe because that's the only space left."

"No," I said. "It's because you're painting a picture."

The Bear in the Plum Tree

"I knew I should have picked those plums," Nancy said.

"But think of the adventure we had," I said.

It *was* an adventure. I wouldn't have missed it for anything. How often do you see a bear right there in the moonlight, right outside your picture window?

It started when Nancy and her husband had to leave town. They needed somebody to babysit the house because of their dogs and cats. Mel said we'd do it, and I said fine.

Now, Nancy and Clarence live in Rattlesnake Canyon, outside of the city limits. It's beautiful up there. The pine trees and the larch trees come right down to your back garden.

And of course the bears come down too. Well, not very often. Usually you get deer, sometimes a skunk.

Mel and I had supper, fed the animals, read a while, then went to bed. At midnight I was awakened by a tremendous commotion. All the dogs in the neighborhood were barking. I flew out of bed, crept downstairs and looked out the kitchen window. It's a picture-glass window that faces the woods. It also faces a copse (I like that word) of plum trees. What's a copse of plum trees? A bunch—that's what it is. A bunch, a group.

Now, these plum trees of the Wendel's aren't much to speak about. They're old and small and scrawny, but they do give plums—fat, purple, prune-type plums.

The trees are square in front of the picture window. I knew something was going on around those plum trees because a circle of dogs was visible in the moonlight.

Suddenly I saw the trees shaking. The boughs were lashing back and forth. "Good heavens!" I said, "There's a bear up in the plum trees."

I flew back upstairs and woke up my husband. "A bear! A bear!" I said. "There's a bear in the plum trees!"

Mel flew out of bed, and we rushed downstairs. "I can't see the bear!" I exclaimed. "Where is he?"

"Hey," Mel said, "we can turn on the spotlight." We did and there was the bear. Oh, what a sight! A big, fat, shaggy brown bear. Not a grizzly. Oh no. Just a big, fat, shaggy brown bear.

But he didn't look brown in the moonlight and the spotlight. He looked silver. He looked beautiful. His head was as big as a house. And so perfectly bear-like.

Well, what did you expect—all our friends said the next day—a bear is a bear—it looks like a bear. But I'd never seen one so close before.

The sight lasted only a second. Then the bear backed down out of the plum trees and ambled off toward the woods. All that was left were barking dogs.

We snapped off the spotlight, but we didn't go back to bed for quite a while. Because there was more left than just the dogs barking. There was a magic feeling—a mysterious feeling—a feeling that there still are "things out there in the night."

We picked the plums the next day, to save wear and tear on the trees. But we left the broken twigs. To remind us.

How To Make
Ready for Winter

Thud! Something fell out of a pine tree on my head. I was walking in the Helena National Forest. Crash Bang! This was getting serious. I looked up. A squirrel was harvesting pine cones. Barely after Labor Day—I was walking in shorts, but the squirrels had received the message: Make ready for winter.

We're doing the same, I said to my husband. Even this hiking in the woods, in the red and yellow of autumn. We have to store up golden days for the long dark ahead. That's what fall is for—to get ready for winter. Animals store up fat. You and I have to store up warmth and color. We have to rev up our hearts and souls in case it's a hard winter.

My Get-Ready-for-Winter List

1) My number one revving up is exactly that—hiking in the fall woods, admiring, exclaiming, feeling the heat and color seep into my bones.

2) Second is harvesting. I think everyone should harvest something, even if you don't have a garden. Dig potatoes or shell corn for the chickens. What am I thinking of? I'm back in the '30s. Who shells corn for the chickens today? You feed them Vita-Mix #4 or something. But the idea is to lay your hands on produce from the growing earth. Gather, harvest, store . . .

If nothing else, pick rose hips, which are the red-orange fruits of the rose bush—either wild or in a garden. All rose hips are edible and a very fine source of vitamin C.

3) Catch a falling leaf and press it in a book.

4) Now I come to what might be the most important part of my Get-Ready-for-Winter List. Right now while the blood is warm in your veins, hot from all the red and yellow and gold—start a project.

It can concern yourself—health, wealth, wisdom—that type, but I'd rather we all got involved in a community project, a common-good type of project. It could even be global. Peace with a capital P. Hunger with a capital H. Yes, I really think the project should be bigger than yourself.

5) Go to the library and take out a book on ideas, something BIG. Say to yourself, "I will expand my thinking." At the very least, you can go out to dinner and astound everyone with your *erudition*.

6) Buy long underwear. Yes, this is the year, even if you're 82. You can buy such pretty longjohns these days—flowered and soft, not like the oldtime, rough, heavy, scratchy stuff. This modern kind is like wrapping yourself in a cloud. Try it. Then, this winter, instead of turning up the heat, slip into your underwear. You can wear nylon on top if you wish. You'll still be warm.

7) Sew a nightcap. Put it on and you can sleep with the windows open. You'll feel much more alive in the morning.

8) Buy an old, white, fuzzy coat—from a rummage sale or a thrift shop—to use as a bathrobe. Most bathrobes aren't worth buying. They're very pretty, but they're no good as far as real warmth goes. If you have to get up in the early morning with the heat turned off, you want something old and big and voluptuously soft and warm. You can even get up in the middle of the night, and you won't catch pneumonia. I couldn't live without my old, white, fuzzy coat.

9) Walk tenderly in the first snowfall. Later on you can shovel and storm and cuss and bemoan. But the first snow is like a newborn baby—so clean and soft. It makes the world newborn. Walk gently in that first snow.

10) This is a serious New Year's Resolution—to be made now. Say to yourself: "I will do something to hold the world together." This is not a simple thing because you have to ask yourself what is causing it to fly apart. What's behind the unrest? Is it greed on some people's part? Is it fear on others? Is everything connected? Ah, that's something to think about.

Frolicking in the Snow—Grandly

I put on my snowshoes and went way out of town, in the woods. I wanted to celebrate snow but I was a little apprehensive: *Should* I celebrate snow when it's such a hardship for so many people?

Maybe snow should fall only on ski resorts, mountain tops and high valleys where it holds moisture for spring. I thought this over and then I laughed. How audacious. Like that line I read in an article: It said we have to use pesticides and herbicides to train nature away from crops.

Train nature! Incredible! But here I was doing the same. Snow, don't fall in the middle of our civilized lives. Fall out there—in your own domain!

Well, in a way—with snowshoes—you are in snow's domain. Even if you're not good at it. I was walking bowlegged and pigeon-toed. I tripped over my own feet. But I was out in a vast expanse of white. Even the pine woods were covered with snow. It was a Christmas card all around me. No one need send me a Christmas card—if you want to say hello, write it on a grocery bag, with a pencil.

The snow kept falling off the trees in huge globs, sometimes right on my head. And new snow was falling—softly, in big flakes. I held out my mittens and caught the flakes. Like a child.

Well, once in a while you have to throw everything up in the air and frolic. That's what I did—grandly. I frolicked in the snow. Made circles, fell down, saw a redheaded woodpecker. He was so beautiful. Snow showered from the tree as that bird pounded away. I always wonder how come woodpeckers don't get headaches. He made a powerful lot of noise. It reverberated in the quiet woods.

The shadows started to lengthen. I turned and went home, brushed off the snow, hung up the snowshoes. The house felt good; the heat felt good. I was back in my civilized life but for a little while I was a black-tailed fox playing in the snow.

Waxwings in the Crabapple Tree

I was on my way to the university when suddenly I was in a cloud of waxwings. I stopped walking and stood still in the snow. "What are you eating now?" I said. "You've already finished the mountain-ash berries."

The birds swooped over to a large maple tree and sat in the bare branches. The tree looked like a candelabra. That's the way waxwings sit in a winter tree. They outline the top branches and you could draw a picture of it.

Because I didn't move a muscle, the birds came down out of the maple tree and moved to the crabapple tree. Well, well, I thought—everything has its turn. Now it's the crabapples.

Those little apples had been on the tree since September. They had frozen and thawed, frozen and thawed—through sleet and snow, rain and wind—waiting for a destiny.

At 10:30 a.m. on the last Tuesday in January the hour came. There was a rendezvous between a flock of waxwings and a crabapple tree.

> *Time, temperature, chemical composition,*
> *perhaps even a turning of the stars,*
> *all came into position*
> *and a flock of waxwings somewhere in space*
> *set their gyroscope and landed on Gerald Avenue*
> *in Missoula, Montana,*
> *to keep a rendezvous with a crabapple tree.*

And Kim Williams was late for her appointment. I had to be because I couldn't move. I was outside the fence of this backyard, standing in the snow. Inside was the crabapple tree. The branches were covered with birds, and the ground was covered with birds. There was a gray carpet of birds on the ground. They were eating the fruit that had fallen off the tree. Some had fallen because the birds knocked it off, and some had fallen because with all the freezing and thawing, the crabapples had turned into mush. A rusty, brown mush lying on the snow.

Waxwings are not quiet. There is a constant sibilance as they eat. A sort of *ssst* sound, as though they were hissing at each other, but I know they're talking. They're friendly birds, and they talk to each other, and they travel in huge flocks.

I stood in the snow and listened. The soft sibilance blended in with the quiet winter sun. I saw my shadow very faintly on the snow.

The birds were wary. They darted and skipped, turning their heads from one side to the other. I lifted my hand and the flock rose in a cloud to spread over the maple tree. A passing car lifted a larger cloud. Birds scattered like chaff in the wind.

And I scattered because I was already late. But I stopped in the next block to sample a crabapple. I had to see what those little apples were like after being frozen and thawed dozens of times. I pulled an apple from the tree, rubbed it in the snow and ate it. It was delicious. It was a pickled crabapple, pickled right there on the tree. The acid had turned into sugar, or it had fermented into cider—perhaps hard cider.

So now we know the destiny of crabapples. They turn into cider preserved in little balls on the tree until something sends a message to the waxwings and they come swooping from somewhere—to feast and to amaze the passersby.

I'm a Night Watcher

What was I doing up at midnight? And standing outside the house? In the snow and cold? When I know very well that early to bed and early to rise is what makes the world go round?

"Hemingway was at his desk, writing, at six in the morning," Mel tells me regularly. "Standing up."

Did Hemingway write standing up? It doesn't matter. The point is that dawn is a marvelous time of day.

So what was I doing abroad at midnight? Well, not really abroad. I was only outside the door.

But I left the warmth of the house. And the light. In fact, I turned off all the lights in the house before I went outside. I could say I was up because it was full moon, the night was white and I was writing poetic lines:

> Live in this moonbright night.
> Live in this white light.

But the truth is I love all nights. I never go to bed without going outside and looking up at the sky: the moon, the stars, clouds.

I wish I had a two- or three-story house to *really* watch the night. I need Robinson Jeffers' tower on the beach at Carmel. I saw it once. He wrote poetry there. What a place to watch the night!

I have to do it in my driveway. There is one exact spot where the neighbors' yard lights are invisible. I know yard lights are insurance policies—very necessary, but they do (forgive me) ruin the night.

Was night ever a friend? Maybe never. Highwaymen and cat burglars stalk the night.

And could I go to the wilderness and spend a night alone? I can't even sleep out under the stars when Mel is right beside me. On every camping trip I drag my sleeping bag outside the tent. "I'm going to sleep under the stars," I say to Mel. Two rustles in the underbrush—a chipmunk no doubt—and I drag my sleeping bag inside.

This little spot of night in my driveway may be all I can cope with. I went into the house and I went out again, letting in the cold, letting out the heat. The snowbanks were high. Everything was quiet and white. I said grandly, "This night is mine."

Should I have said that, when I had only this little spot of night?

But maybe people do say that, even city people with only a tiny spot on a fire escape. You seem to be able to own the night. You can't own the day. It's bright. It's noisy.

Night is soft and quiet. It doesn't ask anything of you. Daylight says we must be up and doing, like Eleanor Roosevelt. Night doesn't say that. Night says let it be. Let civilization slow down like a flywheel coming to a sighing halt. Slow down. Just be.

Surviving

My child, *if it is your fate*
to live in a spaceship on Mars,
you must put a silver bow in your hair
and go, my child. Full speed ahead
to outer space and a steak dinner
made from one-celled yeast.

But there'll always be a Lloyd Rich
who walked into the Garden Show
at Chicago's McCormick Palace
carrying a sassafras walking stick.
He handed me a piece of acorn bread
from out of his buckskin pouch.
He doffed his coonskin cap and said,
"How do you do?"

Some Of Us Will Emulate Euell Gibbons. Some Of Us Will Have Less Success Than Others.

When Lloyd Rich said to me, "How do you do?" I should have answered straight out, "I don't do as well as you do, Lloyd Rich."

I've never made acorn bread. I don't have a buckskin pouch or a coonskin cap.

And I burned the Jerusalem artichoke coffee. After my sweet husband kindly scrubbed and ground up four pounds of the chokes. The house was filled with smoke, and we never got to try one spoonful of "non-coffee coffee."

You live in the middle of Chicago, Lloyd. I live in the suburbs of this little city called Missoula. We're not in log cabins. I'll tell you why I'm not. Because only half of me wants to live in a log cabin, snowshoe to town, eat sourdough pancakes. The other half wants to walk to the university.

Lloyd, are we the urban wild? The suburban wild? But we could survive, couldn't we? I don't mean gun-type surviving—those people dug in underground with camouflage clothes and Winchesters.

Lloyd, we're the Euell Gibbons type. Although I'll have to tell Euell when I see him that I didn't measure up.

Oh, I know the wild plants of the area. I even know the Latin names. Trixie says I know them too well. She said to me when I showed her the biscuit root Lewis and Clark ate, "They [she meant the Gun-type Survivalists] will put you in a cage and hand you plants one by one and make you identify them."

Dear Euell Gibbons, how did you do it? I'm always a dollar short and a day behind. I teach the edible-wild-plants course, and then my students get all the mushrooms and the wild asparagus and I have to go buy mine in the market.

"I know why," Trixie says. "You're not up at dawn."

How can I be up at dawn when I'm standing in the moonlight at midnight? Never mind. Let all my fiascos follow me after.

> *If things are not perfection,*
> *join my Exclaim and Admire Club.*
> *We walk and talk.*
> *The river runs.*
> *There are clouds in the sky.*

Will you agree, Lloyd? And you, Euell Gibbons? Thank you.

Euell Gibbons, I should have had your books when I was five. On our old farm we had dandelions all over the place but nobody in my family—nor the neighbors—was eating them. We didn't eat the rose hips either and certainly we were short of vitamin C. Who had oranges in those days?

When people ask me, "Why should I know about edible wild plants? The stores are full of fruit and vegetables from all over the world," I answer, "In an emergency you could survive." But there are other reasons, aren't there, Lloyd Rich? How about UNEXPECTED JOYS?

> *I pounce on wild edibles. I stalk.*
> *Euell Gibbons, you were right when you said*
> *STALKING THE WILD ASPARAGUS.*
> *One does stalk.*
> *One prowls, one lurks. And when one finds,*
> *one has the right to be a child again,*
> *to shriek and holler and jump up and down.*
> *It is permitted*
> *with morels and wild asparagus*
> *and large Hungry Horse huckleberries.*
> *Eureka! I dine tonight!*

Well, sometimes you don't dine until midnight. Eating from the wild is not like going to a fast-food emporium.

"Let's make cattail pancakes," I said to Trixie.

"Good," she said. "That's what I like about your edible-plants course. We live free, we live off the land."

We got in her car and drove to the country for the cattail roots. It was 10 miles going and 10 miles coming back, so we had to stop at a drive-in for lunch.

We arrived home and started to make the cattail flour. The book said, "Boil the roots into a starchy gruel and dry in a 175° oven. After the gruel is dry, remove the long fibrous hairs and you have flour."

We also had a full day's work. First we had to pick over the roots and discard all the ones that were rotting or had been chewed on by muskrats or other denizens of the deep. Then we had to wash and skin our loot. If you leave the skins on, you get too much of the bitter taste. Then we had to pound the roots with a mallet so the cooking time would be shortened.

We tried just rubbing the pounded roots in a bucket of water. Some people get the flour that way—just working the starch out of the fiber. All we got out of that operation was red, raw knuckles.

We cooked the crushed roots for two hours then poured the mess into cookie pans and put it in the oven. When it was dry (and the house damp), we sifted the fibers out of the flour. At 10 p.m. we had a cupful of flour. Not white flour—it was a shade of brownish gray.

"Now we are ready to go into production on the pancakes," Trixie said. "Read the recipe."

"One cup of light cream," I said. "Three eggs, six tablespoons melted butter—"

"Heavenly days!" Trixie screamed. "What cookbook are you using? We don't need the Cordon Bleu."

"This recipe is in the wild cookbook," I said, "and that's what it calls for: one cup . . . "

"Stop! Stop!" Trixie yelled. "I can't stand it!"

But it was too late to stop. Our families were waiting for cattail pancakes.

It was midnight when we ate, so we called the meal midnight supper.

"How were the cattail pancakes?" my edible-wild-plants class asked the next day.

"Excellent," I said.

Trixie groaned. "Living free . . . " she mumbled.

Our potluck at the end of the class went much better. I have to face it—I am not the world's best cook. My students are always the ones who produce something memorable. I cluck like a mother hen. I try valiantly, but it's like the time I made raisin bread in competition with Lucy in South America. Hers was light and airy. Mine was fed to the cocker spaniel and *she* threw up on the floor.

My main responsibility at the potluck was to check out the ingredients. That's the primary rule of eating wild plants: Don't eat anything you aren't 100 percent sure of. We looked over every stem of lamb's quarter. We examined every berry. We made spore prints of the mushrooms. You have to be very careful with mushrooms. "Don't poison yourself for 50 cents," I say to my students. "That's all a can of mushrooms costs in the supermarket."

But my class studied, and they knew what they were doing. We checked everything and had a gourmet feast.

We started with cattail shoots, the young hearts of the new plants, so tender we ate them raw with herb mayonnaise.

Then we had a soup made of daylily tubers. We didn't find these tubers in the wild. One of the students had a patch on her property. She dug up enough roots to make a cream soup. It was delicious. Daylilies have been used for food for centuries.

We had baked trout from the Blackfoot River. Nice, crispy rainbow trout. We had chickweed salad. Everyone has chickweed in his garden. It's a weed—a common, ordinary weed. But mix that chickweed with new young lamb's quarter and some parsley and chives and a good homemade dressing and you have a salad full of vitamins and fresh as a summer morning.

What would you think of creamed nettles as a vegetable? Very good if the nettles are new and young.

Now here's a real surprise. Thistle stalks. One lady peeled thistle stalks and made a casserole. It tasted just like cooked celery.

I brought some moose meat chili. This wasn't the season for game, but a friend gave me the moose meat from her freezer, because I'd never had any and I said I'd like to taste it. I made it into chili with beans and tomatoes. It was eaten down to the last smidgin.

For bread we had a whole-wheat loaf kneaded with sunflower seeds and dandelion petals. The dandelion petals were for fun. You have to have fun at any gathering.

Dessert was a serviceberry torte and a rhubarb pie. Now, rhubarb isn't a wild plant, but I never did say we had to eat 100 percent wild foods. I don't think we should. I consider wild foods a delicacy, an exotic taste. Something to give us a touch of times past, of a life gone by, when the pioneers and Indians lived off the land.

We can't go back to that today. We're a nation of over 235,000,000 people. Of course in an emergency—if you're lost in the wilderness—then you live off the land. But otherwise, "Just taste," I say to my students, "Enjoy just a little and leave the rest for the birds and wild animals."

The potluck finished with mint tea in the shade of a Ponderosa pine. Lloyd, we should have had acorn bread. Euell, we didn't have dandelion wine. But you would have been proud of us. Nobody got sick either.

Edgar Brooks' Garbage Garden

Edgar Brooks, are you a connection between the edible wild and the cultivated garden? Your garden certainly isn't what people expect. In fact, you were almost run out of town. "Your garden's an eyesore," the city fathers said. "It's a garbage garden."

I met Edgar Brooks when I wrote a piece for our local paper saying, "Let's explore the idea of exchanging manicured lawns for natural prairies."

Of course I received some strong replies. One writer made a whole short story. He had dolls and children and puppy dogs lost in waist-high buffalo grass, and then he had a prairie fire threatening to burn down the town.

Another letter had a neighbor looking out his front window and seeing a cornfield where there used to be a manicured front lawn. "Oh my god," he says to his wife. "When the wind blows, all that loose dirt will come flying into our house and we'll have bees and ants, and next fall a raccoon will burrow under our foundation."

Edgar Brooks wrote, "Why dig up the ground at all? I say just pile organic material on top and plant vegetables."

He sent me a picture of a Hubbard squash so big it almost fell off the stone fence it was sitting on.

People who believe in mulch and compost marvel at what Edgar accomplished on a propery situated on top of a cinder bed left over from an abandoned railroad.

Instead of digging up the cinder bed and bringing in topsoil, Edgar chose to build soil on top of the cinder bed. "Bring me your cornstalks and grass clippings and straw," he said to his friends.

What caused the uproar in the town was the suspicion that Edgar's friends brought not only grass clippings, straw and cornstalks but also ordinary garbage.

I will admit that the day I was there I saw a ballpoint pen sticking out of the soil. But the soil was a foot thick—black, rich-looking, spongy. I could see where Edgar's vegetables and flowers would be well protected against summer drought.

Edgar had been building soil on top of his cinder bed for 12 years. He did not turn the compost under. "Nature doesn't turn its leaves and dried grass under," he stated.

Edgar also used manure and sludge. The sludge came from the town's sewage-treatment plant.

Potatoes were always the first crop after a load of new mulch was added to the garden. This was because potato plants can anchor themselves in loose material. Edgar had a photograph of a little girl holding a four-and-a-half-pound potato. The caption on the picture read, "This potato grew in 15 inches of leaves."

Of course that was exactly the sore point with the neighbors. They were not accustomed to seeing potatoes growing out of a pile of leaves. And how about the straw blowing in the wind? How about the fire hazard?

Luckily, by the time the city fathers were at the height of their campaign to oust Edgar he didn't have much loose material blowing in the wind. He had enough soil to anchor the new loads of straw and hay and—yes—potato peelings, old cabbage, coffee grounds.

And he had friends. The garden-club ladies were asking him to give talks. Edgar scolded them for keeping their lawns too neat, for sweeping up all the leaves and putting them in the trash can. *That library lawn has been kept so clean for so many years,* he wrote in a letter to the editor of the local newspaper, *I will bet those two earthworms the schoolchildren dropped in the soil by the rose bush will have a hard time surviving.*

"Bring me your leaves if you won't make compost out of them," Edgar said to the ladies.

He sent a letter to Appalachia, to the coal-mining companies. *You can build soil on top of those slag piles,* he wrote. *Save all your cornstalks and rotted hay and dried leaves.*

And garbage? Will trains someday haul coal one way from Appalachia and garbage the other?

Edgar, you're like mulching pioneer Ruth Stout. (She was written up in *Organic Gardening* magazine.) Ruth got tired of waiting for the Rototiller man, so she just put straw on her garden and hid the seeds underneath. She saved all the sprouted potatoes and hid them under the straw too. Everything grew and produced.

And wasn't there a man down South who dropped turnip seeds in vacant lots like Johnny Appleseed? Anybody could come and harvest turnip greens in the spring and turnip roots in the fall.

In Australia there's a Tagari community that says, "Out with the plough. Let's go to Permanent Agriculture. Let's grow permanent plants, trees, shrubs—and let's surround them with fish ponds and beehives."

That's for me—Permanent Agriculture.

"I want to come and see your garden," an acquaintance said. "I bet it's huge."

"It is," I said. "It covers the whole Missoula valley."

Am I a throwback to the hunter-gatherer cultures? No. I think it was my not-too-fortunate re-entry into gardening after I left the old farm and took up city ways and then had to relearn gardening. I relearned it in South America, in a city of 3,000,000.

If you can imagine, I had to go find a worm. Like Edgar Brooks' library lawn, our garden was so clean it didn't have worms. I had to go get some from a friend. In a city of 3,000,000 I went across town on the bus and came back on the bus with a plastic bag full of live worms.

I put the worms in our compost pile. Actually it was a compost hole, and a very peculiar one. One night I went out to dump some orange peels into the hole and I had to run back to the house to get Mel. "Come and listen," I said. "The compost hole is alive. It's chomping and gnawing and crunching."

Mel came and then all the dinner-guests came. (We were having a dinner party—a serious dinner party. Mel's boss was in town. I'd baked two kinds of pie. The dinner guests were dressed up—the ladies in high heels, silk dresses and pearl necklaces.)

There we were—all of us—dressed up and standing around that

compost hole, in the moonlight. It was a moonlit night, so we could see, but there wasn't anything to see.

But we could hear the crunching.

"What's in that hole?" Mel's boss asked.

"Just worms," I said.

"Worms don't make noise," Mr. Ward said. "You must have some terrible monster in that hole—buried alive, eating away."

The guests were delighted. After that, whenever we had a dinner party everyone wanted to go and listen to our compost. After dark. That's when the compost was the noisiest. The worms or bugs—or whatever—were all chewing and crunching and gnawing.

It became tremendous entertainment, but it never led to a really great garden. I fell into another disaster. When the garden filled up with weeds—maybe from that compost hole—maybe from the cow manure I dragged home by the gunnysack from our weekend fishing trips—I listened to my Tom Sawyer-sidekick Lucy. "We need chickens," she said. "Three chickens will keep the garden clean."

Would anyone believe it possible for three small chickens to eat up a whole garden? These three did. On top of pure wheat twice a day, plus all the vegetable scraps from the house.

Those chickens never stopped eating. They mowed the lawn like a lawnmower. I had to let the gardener go. How can you have a gardener if you don't have a garden?

Those bottomless pits of voracity ate the petunias, the pansies, the ferns, the veronica, the salvia, the balsam, the daisies—everything. I had a patch of trailing myrtle. I swear those chickens sat and waited for a new shoot to come up so they could snatch it.

I had to call up the garden club and say, "Please don't come for a visit. There's nothing here."

Survival Quiz for Cold Winters and Hot Summers

Would you survive the following?

1) What would I do if the electricity went off for three days?

2) Do I know how to preserve food other than refrigerating it?

3) Do I own clothes that would keep me warm if the heat went off?

4) Can I actually patch a coat or darn socks?

5) Do I know enough about home remedies to carry on without a drugstore?

6) Could I walk five miles if I had to?

7) Am I on good terms with enough friends or relatives to be part of a group in tough times?

8) Could I use barter if I had to?

9) Could I live on five gallons of water a day?

10) Could I live without a flush toilet?

Did you just say, "Stop! I'm fainting!"?

How Basic Can We Get?

Cindy Ort, you have three children and you moved from the city to a run-down farm. You could manage. "I'd never even seen raw spinach until I grew some," you wrote. "The table we eat from was made from three old oak planks my husband snitched from our barn."

Cindy wrote they had no electricity in the "funky old log cabin." They had a battery-powered radio. They sawed their wood by hand, grew a large garden and stored the produce in a root cellar.

Sibyl the cow and 13 goats supplied milk, cheese and butter. Cindy made yogurt by the gallon.

She kept chickens.

She also said, "We can watch the sun set through our west wall where the chinking cracked open."

Cindy, how much water do you use per person per day? Do you figure five gallons apiece? That's what Mavis McKelvey figured when she lived in an A-frame on an abandoned farm in Wisconsin. "If you have to carry your water, you can live on five gallons a day."

"Cutting wood is the big job," Mavis said. "It can panic you how fast the wood supply dwindles."

When Will Kerling went to live in the Rattlesnake Wilderness "to think, to study, to take pictures," he had all the wood and water he wanted. It was food, just plain food, he had to think about. When you carry all your supplies on your back for a month at a time, you ration closely. And you also remember everything you ever learned about edible wild plants.

Will was already in practice. He once "lived off the land" for four days while on a backpacking trip with my husband. The two carried a full supply of food on their backs, but Will decided to eat none of his. "I'm going to see if I can do it," he said. "Live off the land."

He did. He carried all that food on his back and ate not one bite of it. He ate 18 different wild foods. Fish, of course, but also frog legs and snails. Mushrooms, both raw and cooked. Then 14 wild plants—greens, roots, berries. Will didn't get sick, and he didn't lose any more weight than he did on an ordinary trip.

Now, I don't advocate this at all. You could get a terrible stomachache. Yes, people have lived for weeks on just one kind of wild berry or root. An explorer in what is now Yellowstone National Park was thrown from his horse into a thistle patch. The thistle patch is the best thing that could have happened to him because his glasses were broken and he couldn't see, but he could recognize thistles— ouch!—and he ate thistle roots until he was rescued.

One of my students told me about a Marine who crashed his plane in a cattail swamp and lived for 10 days on cattail roots. The student ended the story with, "and he was fatter when he was picked up than when he crashed." I don't know whether to believe this story or not. Cattail roots aren't that good.

A group of explorers in Canada survived on rose hips (the fruit of rose bushes). In an emergency anything is possible. However, I think if you're lost for only one or two days the best advice is:

> *Don't eat anything,*
> *don't drink anything,*
> *don't move.*
> *Somebody will find you.*

Will Kerling ate well-balanced meals on his month-long stays in the Rattlesnake. He carried a lot of bulgur wheat, so he didn't have to dig up roots. I was glad to hear that. Can you imagine all the holes in the ground if we all started rooting around like gophers or ground squirrels?

Will mixed his bulgur wheat with fish and wild greens. "I'm glad I knew about wild greens," he said. "I figure I got all my vitamin C that way."

Nobody in the whole world should ever have had scurvy. All the primitive peoples knew about green plants.

Will, you caught your fish in a mountain lake. Cindy and Dave grow theirs. Cindy's last letter said, "Dave's at the pond catching catfish for supper."

Cindy, that's Permanent Agriculture. Do you have a beehive suspended over the pond so the worn-out bees can fall into the wate· and be re-cycled into fish?

My Survival Shelf

At first I didn't have a label on the shelf. I just put things on it, the kinds of things one would use in an emergency—when the electricity goes off or a blizzard maroons the town. But now this top lefthand shelf in the basement is official. It is the Survival Shelf, and it has a neatly typed label glued to the frame.

Some of the things on the shelf are very sensible and some are rather peculiar, but they're all there to lessen stress and strain in times of emergency.

If winters are going to keep on being as tough as the ones we're having, I think everyone could use a Survival Shelf.

Many of our ideas about food, shelter and clothing need some adjustment. Take clothes for instance. Many people have gone entirely to synthetic fibers. No ironing, lightweight, never shrink or fade. That's fine, but if the heat goes off or your fuel supply is low and you want to turn the thermostat to 62, you'll find there's nothing to compare with good old-fashioned wool. Cotton next to your skin and wool on top. Layers of wool. It doesn't matter if your sweaters are old or your coat is out of style. Put them there on that Survival Shelf.

I have a pair of 100 percent wool slacks, lined. They're heavy and not too comfortable. I'm not wearing them right now, but they're on that shelf. If the heat went off in our house, I'd head for the shelf and take down the wool slacks, two old sweaters and an old coat.

I always wear heavy socks, warm caps and scarves, so they're right in my closet. I'm glad to see more people are wearing caps and scarves. Everyone should know that you can lose a lot of heat through your head.

We keep both a kerosene and a gasoline lamp on the shelf. If the electricity goes off, a candle may be romantic and quite adequate for a short period, but a lamp is safer and more satisfactory for any extended period of time.

How about food ideas? Canned goods of course—everyone knows about those—but have you considered dried food? You can live for months on dried food. If you can't get to the grocery store, you won't need to panic. You can have dried fruit, vegetables, meat and milk.

Don't forget the grains and legumes—rice, beans, peas, lentils, wheat, barley, rolled oats. You'll want sprouting material—a variety of seeds so you can have a continual supply of fresh sprouts. Nuts in the shell will keep for a long time.

I'm going to put some notebooks on the shelf too. Some have recipes and some have—well, here's the label—*Things to do if marooned at 30 below.* You have to do more than just survive. You have to keep your spirits up. You have to have some fun.

Suppose the TV went off. Goodness gracious, could we even survive? So the Survival Shelf needs a Scrabble set, some jigsaw puzzles, a crossword book. (Mel loves crossword puzzles.) I need paper and pencil. Other people need a drawing pad. Checkers and backgammon too. A poetry book to read out loud. A book of plays, also to read out loud.

A jump rope. You need exercise even if you are marooned inside a house.

Tucked away somewhere on the shelf you need something that makes you laugh: a book, some cartoons, a stuffed frog with one eye missing, a letter from a five-year-old nephew.

Maybe your family scrapbook. If a picture of Uncle John in his long underwear will make you laugh, put it on the Survival Shelf. Treasure it. I'm smiling just thinking about it.

Wanted: Apples with Worms in Them

"Here's a sticker for your front door," Trixie said. On the sticker was printed, *Wanted: Apples with Worms in Them.* I laughed out loud because that's what I'd been saying all summer: "I love apples with worms in them. Just give me your alley apples, worms and all. I'll make apple juice and apple butter. Like the canary in the mine in the old days—it's a sign things are safe."

(I used to say *road apples,* but Trixie cured me of that. She's a native Montanan. "You know what road apples are? They're what horses leave behind.")

Until I was 17 years old and went off to college I didn't know you could have an apple without a worm in it. On our old farm we never sprayed anything. Well, we couldn't afford it to begin with, and actually, before World War II there weren't as many chemicals available. I can remember picking potato bugs by hand. Still, we managed to have a crop of potatoes every year.

We had cherries without spraying. We had plums and peaches and many kinds of apples and pears. Oh, I'm sure some years one or two fruit crops failed entirely. Maybe one year the bugs got every peach, but then we ate plums or apples or strawberries. Somehow the bugs always left us enough.

Maybe our farm was so far back in the hills it had evolved a balance between bad bugs and good bugs. By not spraying anything, we certainly didn't kill off any of the good bugs.

Also, we had plenty of birds. Well, of course the birds ate some of the fruit. I can remember robins squawking in the top of the cherry tree as if they wanted all of those beautiful black cherries up there. I wanted them too. But that too balanced out. Don't birds eat bugs?

So we had birds and good bugs to keep the bad bugs in check. And isn't that idea coming back nowadays? You no longer expect to wipe out—annihilate—bad bugs. You simply have to keep them in check.

Choose Your Poison

When Pandora's box opened,
out tumbled flies, ants, mosquitoes,
bugs, bacteria, viruses:
all things creepy, crawly
that have plagued mankind
since time began.
But in the middle of the 20th century
we said "Aha! Eureka! We have done it!
We have put the lid on Pandora's box.
Quick Henry! The Flit!"
ZAP this, ZAP that, ZAP every creepy crawly—
every bug, bacterium, virus.
We will eat shiny apples, luscious pears—
walk on grass as green and perfect
as indoor/outdoor carpeting.
We are free we are free we are free—
of nature's malevolence.

But what's on those shiny cherries? Are they shiny from bursting goodness or is it from Krupp's chemical works?

"I didn't buy cherries in the *feria* today," my housekeeper Lucy said. (How could she be so smart so far away in those red-dirt hills of southern Chile?) "I didn't buy the cherries because the man was spraying them with fly toxin."

Z is for ZAPPING
bugs, bacteria, viruses, flies, ants, mosquitoes—
And me and you.

I Make a Vitamin-Pill Test

I had to make the test because of the "nutrition" workshop I was invited to. "This isn't a nutrition workshop," I said. "It's a sell-vitamins workshop."

I know vitamins and minerals are as necessary as air and water. They are magic substances. They keep you healthy. They can even undo harm. If I had any kind of ailment that I thought could possibly be helped by vitamin therapy, I wouldn't hesitate a minute. I really do believe many cases of mental problems, alcohol problems and drug problems can be helped by large doses of vitamins. Cancer too. Maybe arthritis. Many kinds of disease. So I have to state that I am a firm believer in vitamins.

But I became more and more uneasy at the vitamin workshop I attended. "This is a red herring," I said. I didn't say that to the workshop as a whole. Maybe I should have. I said it to Trixie during intermission. "This is BUSINESS AS USUAL," I said. "Eat a candy bar for lunch then swallow a vitamin pill. Full speed ahead with processed food, additives, preservatives, polluted water, polluted air, nuclear plants, sprayed roadsides—take it all in, pop vitamin pills on top and you'll be fine."

It's the old PILE-ON-MORE syndrome, like the advice in grandmother's cookbook: Too much salt in the soup? Add a spoon of sugar and the soup will be fixed up.

I believe that in the first Queen Elizabeth's time, instead of taking a bath, you put perfume on top of the smell. Now we're doing it with vitamin pills.

A friend gave me 13 years of health magazines. "My aunt had them," she said. That was fine, but you know what else this little old lady had? She had her house so full of vitamins, minerals, capsules, pills and ointments that not one closet door closed. That woman must have spent half of her Social Security checks on "nutrition" supplements.

How much is enough? How does one stop? That's what worries me. You start with one pill a day, then you take two, and eventually your house can't hold them all.

And who's back at base one fighting the fight?

> *The dioxin is in the doorway?*
> *Close the door.*
> *Take a zinc capsule.*

To make my test, I bought a year's supply of multi-vitamin pills. I took one pill a day for 365 days, then I quit. I didn't taper off. I just quit cold-turkey.

I expected to come down with a cold or to feel draggy. But I didn't come down with a cold, and I didn't feel draggy. In fact, I felt lighter on my feet. I said to Trixie, "It's because I'm carrying less iron around." The pills I took were "with iron."

Seriously, how am I going to judge this experiment? Evidently I didn't need vitamins. I could even be better off without them. I really do feel lighter on my feet now that I've quit. And I was getting a little tickle in my stomach toward the end of the year. Was I building up iron or something?

Here is where the danger can arise. How many people, when they get a tickle in their stomach, instead of going backward to less, might go forward to more? Straight to the PILE-ON-MORE syndrome: you have this tickle so you add magnesium, then you add phosphorus, then . . . There's no end to the business.

We'll Manage

Is this the same person who once fell out of her evening gown at an embassy ball—this person who makes dandelion salad and walks in 25-cent shoes from the Methodist Church rummage sale?

Yes, it's the same person, and I feel just as good. In fact, I feel better. I never thought that episode would last. It was an unnatural life.

Oh, I adapted. You can adapt to anything. And that's the hope of the future. If necessary, we can adapt to a different way of life.

Now, there might come some marvelous discoveries. Energy, as cheap and plentiful as any we ever had, will come flying out of the sun or the earth or the ocean. We'll learn to deal with pollution; everyone will live in peace; everyone will eat; everyone will have two cars and a camper.

But that may not be the scenario. We might have to live a smaller life, make do with less.

We can cry and weep and wail. Or we can say, "This is it. Let's get on with the business of living."

I think the latter is what we'll do. We'll say: "We had it pretty good. In fact, we had it very good. It was unnatural. Now we're down to an ordinary life. But we're tough. We'll manage."

Politics

Nobody is going to do it but us.
Either WE DO IT
or THEY DO IT
TO US.

Mr. President, Just Raise the Taxes—Period

I mailed the letter to the President. He might never see it, but in a democracy you write letters to the President. I started out in verse form:

> Dear Mr. President:
> Don't give my husband
> a Social Security raise.
>
> Give jobs to the unemployed,
> give a chance to the young,
> see to the poor.
>
> Mel and I have enough.

I didn't want to write a long letter. You don't have to write a lot when you write to the government. Your letter is just a tally. It probably goes into a large computer and is added to the total of LETTERS FOR or LETTERS AGAINST.

My second paragraph was:

> The problem is not the elderly. It's the elderly poor. We have to take care of the elderly poor without fattening the elderly rich.

I liked that last sentence so much I repeated it. But after reading it over I crossed out the word *rich*. Because most people don't consider themselves *rich*. Most people in the United States would call themselves *middle class*.

Still, I do believe many people would give up their raise in Social Security if it meant a little more justice and equality. We can't go on with:

More to the Haves—
Less to the Have-Nots.

After living in South America all those years, I get very worried. It's like a cold wind on my back—the gap between the rich and the poor.

Don't let it get any wider, Mr. President. I really think, Mr. President, people would be willing to pay taxes on all their Social Security—100 percent of it—if it were done on a regular sliding scale like all income tax is, OR SHOULD BE.

Oh dear, I should have added that last paragraph to the letter. My letter stopped way back with *fattening the elderly rich*. This proves you should always let things you write sit and ripen.

I should also have added something about waste in the Pentagon and Congressman junkets and . . . No. You shouldn't blur your edges. Say one thing and say it loud and clear. I shouldn't have even written a letter, especially not in verse. A postcard is what I should have sent:

Look, Mr. President, just raise taxes and do it in a fair and equitable way. Period.

We Are All
Welfare Recipients

WE ARE ALL WELFARE RECIPIENTS
you titled your talk. Dear Mr. Adams,
what an uproar! The fur was flying!
To tell a bunch of frontiersmen
we are all welfare recipients.
"My own mother," you said—
"She lives in subsidized housing.
People who have mortgages—
they have a subsidy on their income tax."
Dear Mr. Adams, I have a friend
who intones, once a week,
"Well, you know, Kim,
them what has, gits."
In the military it's
"Rank hath its privileges."

I'm glad I met you, Trixie, after I heard that talk. How many mothers on AFDC have I known? And certainly no AFDC mothers like you, who are nurses but leave nursing to go back to school when they are divorced and have no visible means of support, as they say.

I said this to you, Trixie, right out. We're good friends and we talk. You said, "Isn't it better I go back to school now? I have half a degree in psychology." You leaned back in your chair and lit a cigarette.

"Trixie, why are you smoking?" I asked.

"Because I have only half a degree in psychology," you answered.

Good thing I didn't speak up. Trixie, I was born in that category of "I walked two miles to school, worked my way through college, took jobs in a laundry and a frozen pea factory, wore bells on my ankle in an Indian hash house, raised myself by my own bootstraps or a skyhook." Now I know. We are all welfare recipients.

My own father—was his job a real job? Did Pop earn his way working on a road crew or was it a makeshift job because the man had seven children and lived on a rock-hill farm that couldn't support a puppy dog?

We children never knew. All we knew was that Pop worked on the road. That is how we always put it: Pop worked on the road. During the summer he stayed home to hay. During spring and fall he worked on the road.

He didn't want to. He had come to this country to be a landowner. And he was. He worked in the steel mills of Pennsylvania before and during the first World War. Somehow he and my mother saved enough money to buy—sight unseen—a piece of land in upper New York state. But the land wasn't a farm. It didn't produce a living.

A neighbor probably introduced Pop to the proper channels to get a job on the road. This neighbor, Clyde Smith, worked on the road all his life. Probably he took Pop along one day and said to someone, "This man needs a job. He can't support his family on that rocky farm he bought."

Maybe it was makework. Maybe they had more people on the road crew than they really needed. Some years I seem to remember Pop had only a few months of work in the whole year.

I don't remember being called a welfare family. Maybe we were. Everyone in our valley was called something. The Freed family were "garbage-eaters." They had the franchise for the garbage from the Taconic State Park concession. What the franchise amounted to was saying *yes* to having a truck dump its load on your property. At school the Freeds ate tell-tale sticky buns for lunch.

Did the Freeds get free corned beef once in a while from the government as we did? I'm sure we didn't tell each other if we did.

The government-issue dresses my family received were as tell-tale as the Freeds' sticky buns. The flowered design was a standard.

The dresses and corned beef were haphazard and a drop in the bucket. Pop's job, even though not steady, was, in a way, very steady. Pop worked. Our father worked. We did not, like the hillbillies, make baskets to sell. We did not cut trees on other people's property and drag them away at night.

Dear Mr. President and Congress: If it is at all possible, use the money you have for the poor to give jobs. Some people will have to receive out-and-out aid—just plain welfare—but a job allows the whole family to stand up straight. "My dad works on the road." That's how you'd say it today.

Of course when I went to Cornell I elevated the job. *Occupation of father*—one form after the other asked. *Road-builder* I wrote. *Bridge-builder* I wrote. By the time I got to South America and a teaching job at the university I wrote *Civil Engineer.*

Please note that, Mr. President. A person can build and amplify, but that person needs a start. With dignity. "My father works."

> *Don't dump on the down and out.*
> *They can't steal enough*
> *to sink the battleship.*
> *It's the rich who have the power*
> *and the plans.*
> *If your grandfather stole 200 grand*
> *you'd never have to lift a finger again.*
>
> *If "Them what has, gits,"*
> *Well, then—*
> *Them what doesn't have*
> *have to "git" the best way they can.*
> *Take back your corn and beans, Juan Perez!*
> *Women, take back the night.*
> *Also the herbs and the babies.*

If you can't be born rich
be born lucky.
If neither,
sue everybody—
the doctor, the hospital, your mother—
for cruel and unusual punishment.

We need basic health for everyone,
not half a dozen artificial hearts.
We are connected—
to corn and beans in Guatemala,
your vacation home,
my electric toothbrush.

Do not save my life with medicines
if you do not give me food.

How I Lost the Election for State Legislature

"Where did those pears come from?" Mel asked.

"I was going door to door," I said. "I rang the doorbell and left a flier. Then I saw this pear tree in the yard. It was loaded. The pears were falling on the ground. 'Are you going to use those pears?' I asked the owner. 'If not, I'd be happy to pick them up.'"

No, that didn't lose me the election.

Was it when I received an invitation signed NO HOST and I looked in the phonebook for a person called N.O. HOST?

No, it wasn't that either. Actually the best person won. By the end of the campaign I was campaigning for him.

I simply wasn't destined for the state legislature.

I tried. I made two casseroles for the Jefferson-Jackson fund-raiser dinner, although I was a bit chagrined when I walked in loaded down and there were the men candidates walking in with their hands in their pockets.

"Are the men bringing casseroles?" I asked my friend June, who was running for clerk and recorder.

"Now you know," she said. "We will also serve the coffee."

I carried the coffee tray on high like Jove's handmaiden. I still lost the election.

But June won. So that's 50 percent, and I got practice in politics and a whole winter's supply of pears and apples.

I also started a new club, the White-Cotton-Socks-Don't-Hide club. It was at the last candidate forum before the primary. This lady in front of me was trying to hide her feet. She was pushing them under the seat of the woman in front of her.

I wrote a note on the back of my agenda and passed it to the lady. I say *lady* because I know that's how she would want to be addressed. She had on a blue polyester suit and Red Cross shoes and her hair was "done."

Then why was she trying to hide her feet? It was because she had on white cotton socks instead of nylon stockings.

"Don't hide your feet," I wrote on the note. "Join my White-Cotton-Socks-Don't-Hide club." I was not being frivolous. It's very serious. You start with white cotton socks, you end with the world.

I took off my girdle in 1965. Now I raise my right hand: "Women of the world, it's more than your bottom that you stuff into a girdle. It's your head."

The People Have To Do It

Want to gamble?
Don't put nickels in a one-armed bandit.
The fastest game in town is
P.P. for Precinct Politics.
"New ideas don't start in Washington,"
our state senator said. "They start
at the grass-roots level.
Politicians jump on the bandwagon
when it's rolling."

Nobody is going to do it but us.

You can't wait for the government,
the system, our leaders.
It comes down to very ordinary people—
you and me.

Letter to Will Kerling in Jail, or 10 Rules for Holding on to Your Head While in Jail for Climbing Over the Fence at a Missile Site

Dear Will,

I'm keeping a copy of these rules because I may need them myself. I once started a play: "When Grandma Walked into the Crematorium . . ."

Now I say—

> *Hey Grandma,*
> *don't walk into the crematorium.*
> *MARCH ON THE PENTAGON!*
> *Who better than us oldies?*
> *What can they do to us?*
> *500 grannies marching on the Pentagon!*
> *Are they going to put us in jail?*
> *They'd have to run to the drugstore —*
> *for Fasteeth, Polident, Maalox, Serutan,*
> *Metamucil, Sominex.*
> *Can you imagine the bill?*
> *And they'd have to fix up*
> *all our ailments. Free.*
> *They couldn't afford us.*

I hope you're writing in your journal, Will. Remember when you spent that winter in the wilderness and you kept a journal? You read parts of it to me. "I met a coyote nose to nose on the trail," you wrote. "At first I thought it was a dog. It was coming along so nonchalantly, right toward me. Then we both stopped, looked at each other, and the coyote veered off the side of the trail."

Remember when the Canada geese talked to you? They circled overhead, went up the drainage and back. You said it sounded just like people talking.

Think about those things while you're waiting for lunch or dinner, Will—or just waiting. Think about ice-fishing with Mel, about hiking up McLeod Peak to see the ladybugs, about working on the Forest Service trails during the summer.

You're halfway through your 90 days. You've written 200 letters; you're studying German; you're exercising every day. You're doing OK, Will. You don't really need my 10 Rules, but pass them on to someone else:

10 Rules for Holding on to Your Head While in Jail for Climbing Over the Fence at a Missile Site

1) Exercise three times a day, until you huff and puff.

2) Go outside as often as permitted. Don't stand still one second of outdoors-time. Walk walk walk.

3) Write in your journal every day. Wasn't it Arnold Bennett who said one must make money out of the worst moments of one's life? Someone might pay you for your journal.

4) Hobnob with someone who has a sense of humor. If you can't find that someone, then you must be the one. Laugh once a day. At least chuckle. At least smile. Maybe a weak grin?

5) Study something very difficult.

6) Read real books, not trash.

7) Squeeze a tennis ball while watching TV or listening to the radio.

8) Write one page each on *The 10 Peak Experiences of My Life So Far.*

9) Write down what will be the high point of each month after you get out of jail—12 high points for the next 12 months. You might find this turning into a kind of chart—"Where do I go from here?"

10) Forgive your pa and ma. It will take time for them to come to terms with this person they don't really know.

For Melanie Who Is Seven

Melanie, take your Magic Marker
(this may be the only magic
that marker will ever do)
and draw a clock,
put the hands at 8:15,
print on the clock THINK PEACE,
paste the clock on the refrigerator door.

At 8:15 every morning and 8:15
every evening
close your eyes and fly
to the clock on the refrigerator door.
This is your contribution
to the future of the world, Melanie.

You and I know
there are good fairies
and there are bad fairies.
The bad fairies are thinking WAR.

But they are few
and you and I are many.
There are refrigerators all over the country;
you and I must draw a clock on every one.
At 8:15 in the morning and 8:15
in the evening
the good fairies will
THINK PEACE.